Joy *and* Hope

IN THE MIDST *of* PAINFUL TRIALS

MICHAEL FULLMER

WESTBOW
PRESS°
A DIVISION OF THOMAS NELSON
& ZONDERVAN

This book is a work of non-fiction. Unless otherwise noted, the author and the publisher make no explicit guarantees as to the accuracy of the information contained in this book and in some cases, names of people and places have been altered to protect their privacy.

WestBow Press books may be ordered through booksellers or by contacting:

WestBow Press
A Division of Thomas Nelson & Zondervan
1663 Liberty Drive
Bloomington, IN 47403
www.westbowpress.com
844-714-3454

Because of the dynamic nature of the Internet, any web addresses or links contained in this book may have changed since publication and may no longer be valid. The views expressed in this work are solely those of the author and do not necessarily reflect the views of the publisher, and the publisher hereby disclaims any responsibility for them.

Any people depicted in stock imagery provided by Getty Images are models, and such images are being used for illustrative purposes only. Certain stock imagery © Getty Images.

Scripture quotations are from the ESV® Bible (The Holy Bible, English Standard Version®), copyright © 2016 by Crossway, a publishing ministry of Good News Publishers. Used by permission. All rights reserved.

ISBN: 978-1-6642-4548-8 (sc)
ISBN: 978-1-6642-4549-5 (hc)
ISBN: 978-1-6642-4547-1 (e)

Library of Congress Control Number: 2021919457

Print information available on the last page.

WestBow Press rev. date: 09/21/2021

Contents

Preface

Roughly fifteen years ago, I was asked to teach a six-week series on insights from God's Word concerning trials and suffering. At the time, my brother, Dan, was in the final stages of a devastating neurological condition known as Lewy body dementia (LBD). It ravaged his body and his genius IQ. In the final stage, it produced hallucinations and ultimately took his life. Given our extremely close relationship, this was devastating to watch. Having walked through this with Dan and his family, I felt somewhat equipped to share some personal insights as our study series unfolded.

What I did not understand at the time was that God was preparing both my wife, Chris, and myself for a long, difficult road still ahead of us. The series of events that followed are discussed in this book. They resulted in deep reflection on such issues as:

- Why is there so much suffering in this world?
- How do we see past the darkness of these moments?
- Is anxiety a sign of weakness in our faith, or is it normal? What can we do with it?
- If God's Word says all things work together for good, why am I going through this?
- What is God's purpose in all of this?
- What is the relationship between trust and peace?
- How do I eventually emerge from this?

Having walked this path, I thoroughly searched the scriptures for answers and reflected on what God has taught us both. While the pain will be felt and tears will be shed, there is good news. God has provided a way to experience both joy and hope, even in the middle of the most difficult trials. I ask that you allow me to take you through our journey and share a story about the love, strength, joy, hope, and peace that we increasingly found as our loving Lord walked with us through some of our most difficult and painful moments.

Chapter 1

—ɯɯ—

THE TREMOR

It was the Fourth of July. The family was gathered for the long-standing tradition of barbequed treats, games, family tales, fireworks, and lots of laughter. Dan, my older brother, and I were in a fierce horseshoe battle against Dad and my younger brother, Greg. I was now in my mid-forties, and the challenge had been going on since my youth. This was what we do as a family on the Fourth. The score was close. Then I caught a glimpse of it, a quick tremor in Dan's left hand. Dad threw next. It was a leaner, but I was totally focused on Dan's left hand. As he reached for his next shoe, I watched. There it was again, the tremor. Dan noticed that I was staring.

Dad and Greg in the Heat of Battle

"What's with your hand?" I asked.

Suddenly all eyes were on Dan's hands.

After a moment of hesitation, Dan shrugged. "Not sure. It started a couple of weeks ago."

"Did you get it checked out?" I persisted.

Looking at the ground, he wanted to ignore me but knew me too well. Finally looking up, he said, "Not yet."

"Dan, it may be nothing, but you need to have a physician look at it."

"I know." He looked down at his hand. "I will."

I thought about his response, *He is going to do what we guys always do, ignore it, and hope it goes away.*

Staring at him, I said, "I'm serious. I'm going to call you every week until you do."

I knew I was being a nudge, but working in the healthcare field, I had seen the long-term effects of conditions that failed to be diagnosed early. Delayed treatment too often impacts the opportunity for a successful resolution. And so, true to my word, I called each week.

Finally, after the third call, he realized I would never cease until he had scheduled an appointment. He went to see his family physician, which led to a referral and visits with a local neurologist. Then came a call with the news.

"Hey, Mike. I just got the results from the neurologist."

I waited, as a conspicuous silence followed.

Dan continued, "I apparently have Parkinson's."

It was the news I was afraid of. Not surprisingly, he sounded a bit down. The news quickly spread to the family. After we all got over the initial shock, we committed to encouraging him and helping him through this, wherever it might take us.

Over the coming months, the symptoms progressed. Dan developed workarounds to keep himself functional. It was hard to watch his physical deterioration. As hard as it was, Dan never lost his smile or upbeat personality We could see, though, that it was taking its toll on Dan and the family. It seemed to be progressing faster than we expected.

One day we stopped by to visit. While Kathy, Dan's wife, and my wife, Chris, visited upstairs, Dan and I sat in the basement talking about an upcoming family event. I noticed Dan taking notes. Now taking notes is often a sign of diligence and careful planning. But not in this case. Dan never took notes. Dan had a genius IQ. He had scored a 1580 out of a possible 1600 on his SAT college entrance exam. If he didn't have a photographic memory, he was close.

"You're taking notes?" I asked.

He just nodded.

"When did you start taking notes?" I asked gently. This seemed so unlike Dan.

Dan and Kathy, the Earlier Years

"I've been having trouble remembering things," he confessed. "I'm not sure what's going on. It's beginning to affect me at work. I am constantly taking notes. I noticed my buddies at work covering for me."

Dan worked for a respected IT company and was often the lead on network projects for its largest key accounts like Johnson & Johnson. It was a mentally demanding field, but Dan was known for his ability to work through difficult issues and solve even the most complex problems. This didn't make sense. Why would Parkinson's have such an effect on his memory? This news deeply troubled me.

Two weeks later, Chris and I were again visiting Dan's house. Our families often hung out together. Dan was more than my brother; he was a best friend. Chris had also developed a very close relationship with Kathy. As we sat with them, they dropped the second bomb.

Dan hesitated. Then looking at Kathy, he shared, "I had a follow-up visit with my neurologist to share my recent memory challenges."

We looked at Dan and then Kathy. She just looked down at the table.

Dan continued, "After a lot of questions and some testing, he sat me down and explained that his original diagnosis of Parkinson's was incorrect. His current assessment is that I actually have a condition called Lewy body dementia." Dan was calm and carefully detailed his conversation with his neurologist. "The symptoms are much like those of Parkinson's and dementia, but they develop at a more rapid pace."

Despite the strong face Dan was putting on, we could see that this was hitting them both hard. Chris and I tried to absorb it all. It was a tough pill to swallow. We all sat quietly for a bit, unsure of what to say.

As I thought about it over the week that followed, I was just not ready to accept it. Dan's neurologist may have been very capable, but there are folks who are experts in these matters. Could his neurologist be wrong? He was once already.

Around this time, I jumped on a plane and headed out to a major medical conference. I had been involved in developing continuing education programs for physicians and other health professionals for roughly a decade. Four years earlier, I had started my own company in the field. I attended this conference to oversee an evening event that our company helped organize. Its goal was to update the physician audience on the latest advances in the diagnosis and management of Alzheimer's.

Immediately after the session, I walked to the front to chat briefly with the faculty chairman, a nationally recognized expert on dementia and Alzheimer's. He was affiliated with Harvard and practiced at Massachusetts General Hospital in Boston. After thanking him for his leadership and a very well-received presentation, I asked if I might share a personal situation. I quickly shared the background on Dan's condition. After carefully and patiently listening to my synopsis, he invited us to visit him in Boston. He planned to have Dan meet with him and his team for the purpose of a second assessment. At last, I was going to get to the bottom of this perplexing clinical situation. I was both excited and hopeful.

Upon my return home, I called Dan to convey what I had been able to arrange. We were both feeling optimistic.

A week later, Dan and I threw our bags in the car and began our journey to Boston. It was a six-hour drive, but it gave us time together, which I always valued. Upon arrival at the neurology department of Massachusetts General Hospital, my contact poked his head into the waiting area, welcomed us both, and briefly explained the schedule for the day. It involved a variety of tests as well as meetings with key members of his staff. It was to be a full day of activity.

As the day progressed and we reached late afternoon, I could see that Dan was beginning to look a bit worn, but he remained upbeat.

At approximately 4:30, my contact, the department head, called us into a private exam room and sat across from us.

At first, he just sat without saying a word. Looking directly at Dan, he finally spoke. "Well, I met with the team, Dan, and reviewed all of the test results. I'm sorry to tell you that your neurologist's diagnosis is correct."

Dan and I looked at each other and sank back into our chairs.

The department chair then went on to explain what to expect with Lewy body dementia. "The Parkinsonian-like symptoms will continue to progress, along with the dementia symptoms. The progression will be at a much faster pace than what most patients face with either of these diseases. In the late stages, hallucinations are common. At first, they may appear as shadows in your peripheral vision. In time, however, the images can become quite vivid."

In closing, he shared one final piece of information. He paused for a moment. "You also need to know that the life expectancy is typically around seven years from diagnosis."

Dan was fifty years old at the time.

"I am very sorry to have to share this information with you, Dan. If you have any follow-up questions or if I can help in any way, please don't hesitate to reach out to my office." He handed Dan his card.

It was a quiet ride home. We were both exhausted and deeply disappointed. This was not the outcome I expected. The news about hallucinations and a seven-year life expectancy were both new information. This shocked us to the core. I didn't know what to say to Dan. As I drove, I began to think about Kathy and his children, Jason (Jay) and Lauren. How would they take this? They all adored Dan. I worried about how this news would impact them.

We returned home. The news was shared, and tears were shed. It was a difficult message to convey.

Over the following months and years, the condition began to unfold just as we had been told it would. It was a difficult period for the family. Jay stayed in touch through routine phone calls while he continued his commitment at the Air Force Academy in Colorado. Lauren, while a leading student in her class, turned down her opportunity to live on campus at the university she had selected as her first choice. She instead enrolled in a local college that was commutable. She insisted on being at home to support her mom and dad. Kathy was, as always, the faithful, loving wife, doing whatever was required to support Dan.

Lauren, Dan, Kathy, and Jay

Roughly a year after Dan's diagnosis, the three brothers decided to take a trip to Indianapolis to attend the Indianapolis 500. Dan and Greg had always been huge Indy car race fans. While I had not really followed the sport, the idea of the three of us going on this adventure was exciting. Dan's physical condition had deteriorated, but we all felt we could work through the challenges. So I hitched our twenty-eight-foot travel trailer to our SUV; loaded Dan, Greg, and Greg's wife, Sue, into the car; and began our trek from New Jersey to Indianapolis, Indiana.

It was a long first leg. By around 9:00 that night, we were near Dayton, Ohio. We found a campground and decided to call it a day. I parked the trailer and headed to the public facilities to wash up and get ready for bed. Dan was still able to walk at this point, but his movements were slow and rigid. His posture was hunched over.

As we made our way into the public restroom and shower area, we noticed that the paper towel dispenser was releasing only a couple of inches of towel with each hand wave under the dispenser. Greg and I waved our hands with rapid-fire motions until at last we had a full-sized paper towel.

As Dan made his attempt, the hand motions were in slow motion: a stroke, a pause, a stroke, and a pause.

With barely four inches of towel hanging from the machine,

Dan looked over smiling and said, "You may as well go to bed. This could take a while."

We all just laughed and then did our rapid chops underneath until Dan also had a full towel. From here, we made our way back to the trailer. Greg was the first to arrive. Just short of the trailer steps, he tripped over something.

"What …?" Attempting to regain his balance, he searched through the darkness for the obstacle.

Unfortunately, I was only a step behind him. I stumbled next.

"Whoa! What was that?" I too was looking at the ground surrounded by darkness. Then as I leaned forward and looked down, I noticed a large tree root.

A few minutes later, Dan came along. He did his short shuffling steps, a bit hunched over, face pointing to the ground. As he arrived at the root, Greg and I both turned around and got ready to yell out a warning. Before we could speak, Dan stopped, lifted each foot over the root, and then proceeded in his hunched posture to the trailer steps.

Then, his head swiveled in our direction, and with a huge smile, he said, "See, it does have its advantages." Again, he had us all laughing. Crippled, hunched over, and struggling to walk, he was still that fun-loving, cheerful, smiling brother we all loved.

The trip was so much fun. I gained a greater appreciation for Indy car racing. More importantly, I saw a brother whose body and memory were growing increasingly weak but whose heart was as strong as ever.

As the years passed and the disease continued to progress, we all did our best to adjust to this new normal. Chris and I, like so many family members and friends, were in continued prayer that God would lift this burden and heal my brother. In the meantime, we loved him, supported him, and tried to spend as much time with Dan as possible.

Four years into the Lewy body dementia, as Dan battled ever-increasing symptoms, we found ourselves suddenly faced with another blow to the family, the death of Chris's dad, Pop Ward. Pop had developed ever-troubling symptoms related to coronary artery disease. He fought the battle for a period, but it ultimately took his life.

Mom and Pop Ward

One year after his passing, we got hit with another painful announcement, Kathy had been diagnosed with breast cancer. There had been earlier signs that warranted further testing, but her physician discounted the signs. No further testing had been ordered. She was now in stage four. She was quickly scheduled to begin treatment. Considering how advanced it was, the prognosis was not good. Dan and Kathy's children, Jay and Lauren, were once again shaken to the core.

One year after Kathy's diagnosis, we lost another beloved family member. Chris's mom passed away. She had been diagnosed earlier with kidney cancer. She completed her chemotherapy treatment and seemed to be bouncing back, but sadly the cancer returned. We endured yet another painful loss. She was someone whom we all dearly loved. The trials just kept on coming.

Chris, Our Daughter, Jenn, and Mom Ward

With the loss of Chris's mom and dad still on our hearts, we attempted to focus on supporting Dan and Kathy. Dan continued to regress both physically and mentally (memory). Kathy seemed to be tolerating her treatment well and was quick to divert the attention and support to Dan. With Dan's condition so physically evident, I wonder if we underestimated her own struggles.

As Dan entered his seventh year of the Lewy body dementia, he began experiencing hallucinations. It started as a moving shadow. He said it looked like a mouse running along the baseboard in his periphery. If he turned to look directly at it, the image would disappear.

In the months that followed, the images became more vivid. They were no longer in his periphery and were hard to distinguish from reality. One night, Kathy awoke and noticed that Dan was not in bed. It was after midnight. She went searching for him and found him crouched behind the sofa in the living room. She approached, and he turned toward her.

Putting his finger to his lips, he said, "Shhh!" He pointed across the room.

"Dan ..." Kathy began.

Again, he repeated, "Shhh!" Without another word, he stared across the living room. Finally he whispered, "I'm playing hide-and-seek with the children."

Kathy just looked.

He turned and looked at her, returned his gaze to the living room, and then again turned to Kathy. He paused and then said, "There are no children, are there?"

She just shook her head.

As much as the dementia had robbed him of his short-term memory, his incredible intellect allowed him to continue to analyze situations related to his condition. He assessed them with clarity of thought. He could not remember what he had for breakfast, but we often chatted about clinical situations he had faced. He would dissect them, evaluate what had happened, and then seek a greater understanding of his condition. Many of these conversations started with "It's interesting that ..." I thought to myself, how many individuals, if faced with this situation, would give in to fear and/ or total despair. Dan, by contrast, seemed to be resolved to his condition and was interested in better understanding its path.

Dan in Later Stages, Wheelchair-Bound

This is not to suggest it was not difficult. He had experienced painful trials in his life. He had been to Viet Nam and looked death straight in the face. While there, he watched his fellow platoon members bring his best friend back to camp in pieces on a stretcher after having stepped on a landmine. One can only imagine his pain and grief as he cried out to our mom halfway across the globe.

This current trial ran deep not only for him, but for all those around him who deeply loved him. Yet while he hurt, he showed amazing inner strength. The resolve, I came to understand, had much to do with something that had occurred not long before his diagnosis.

Reflecting on my own life, I had begun to learn about our Lord Jesus at the age of ten while attending a Christian school. I was taught that God existed in three persons: the heavenly Father, Jesus, and the Holy Spirit. I understood that Jesus died a horrific death on the cross out of love for us so our sins could be forgiven. I learned that with this sacrifice, Jesus had paid the price for my sins so that one day I could be with him forever in heaven.

My early years came with challenges. My dad was in the construction field, which took wild swings with each change in the economy. My parents often found themselves on the financial edge. The ups and downs resulted in a never-ending series of moves. By the time I finished my elementary education, I had already attended seven different schools. The result, for me, was a constant struggle for scholastic achievement and a difficult time creating lasting friendships.

Throughout the struggles, I clung to my relationship with the Lord. The Lord was my strength and comforter. The Lord became an integral part of my daily life. As I moved on to high school, my relationship with the Lord continued to grow.

Then came college. This, sadly, led to a decade of drifting. I was all about fun, parties, friends, excessive drinking, and general self-absorption. By my late twenties, I had a growing sense of being completely lost. During my early adult years, I had achieved so many things I had yearned for as a child. I had many friends and had become quite popular within that circle. I had achieved a master's degree with a major in marketing and minor in finance. I had early success in my career and rapidly progressed within a major pharmaceutical firm. By age twenty-nine, I owned my first home.

Were these not the things we all strive for as our goals in life? I still thought of myself as a Christian, but I felt empty and lost.

Now having my attention, the Lord in his mercy began to draw me back to himself. He used ways and people for which I will be eternally grateful. I got involved in a weekly Bible study that opened my eyes to things I had forgotten, did not fully understand, or had never seen before. With each study, I hungered for more. I came to understand that it was not about the accumulation of good deeds, sacraments, and memorized prayers. Rather it is about a loving, growing, devoted relationship with our loving Lord, the very thing I once had but walked away from. It was about Jesus, who willingly left perfection at his Father's side to come to this imperfect world and teach us about perfect love. An then, as if this was not enough, he died an incredibly painful death nailed to a cross delivering the promise of forgiveness and eternal life with him in heaven. He did all this because he loved me that much. My prayers changed from memorized citations to routine discussions and moments of praise and thanks. While I was and clearly am still a work in progress, it changed my life.

For years leading up to Dan's diagnosis, I had attempted to share with Dan these very things that the Lord had patiently taught me. I desperately wanted him to have the same life-changing hope and joy that I had been granted, despite my earlier rebellion. Considering himself a scientist, he would only believe in that which he could see, thoroughly understand, and explain through science. Each time I would share my experiences or invite him to an event at our church, he'd say, "I'm glad this is such a comfort for you. It's just not me."

But God never stops loving or pursuing us. One day in his office, Dan noticed a colleague sitting at his desk reading his Bible after lunch. Dan knew and had a good relationship with this colleague. He did not, however, want to disturb him or ask questions. Each day his colleague would have his lunch and then jump into a time of scripture reading.

Finally Dan's curiosity overtook him. He entered his buddy's office and started a conversation. Then he began asking questions. Over time, each question led to more questions and answers. With each visit, God kept working on Dan's heart until at last he gave it to our Lord Jesus. I was beyond thrilled.

Little did I understand the significance of the timing of this decision. Two years later, Dan was diagnosed with Lewy body dementia. The Lord quickly became his hope, strength, and peace during terrible difficulties and the unimaginable hardships that accompanied this horrible disease. Again, I'm not suggesting that he didn't have times of sadness or discouragement. I am also not saying he didn't have questions. He did, but as we watched him travel this path, Dan clearly found his resolve, strength, and peace in the Lord.

In Dan's last year, I periodically took Fridays off and sat with him on the porch to just talk. On one Friday visit, he asked if I wanted some ice cream. Our entire family was totally addicted to ice cream. I was no exception. Our mom had trained us well.

"Sure," I said enthusiastically.

Kathy brought out a half-gallon of butter pecan (my favorite), two spoons, and two bowls. The carton had been opened but was still two-thirds full. As a sidenote, one of the interesting attributes of this horrible disease is that its victims can consume huge amounts of food without gaining an ounce of weight.

As we continued to talk, I watched Dan ignore the bowls as he began dipping into the ice cream carton with his spoon. Spoonful by spoonful, he continued to drill down into this delightful treat while waxing on in conversation, never missing a beat. In time, I heard him scraping the bottom of the carton while scooping the final remains from the edges.

I was yet to have had single a bite. "Yes, I'd love some ice cream," I finally said, staring at him with a smile.

He hesitated for a moment, looked down at the empty carton, and suddenly realized what he had done. We looked at each other, and then we both burst out laughing. It was a sight to behold: empty carton in his hand, spoon licked clean, and Dan with that goofy grin. I just shook my head, still smiling.

To follow was a period of silence, and then Dan spoke again. He looked straight at me. His eyes locked on mine, and his expression was now very serious. It was to be a conversation that I will never forget.

He said, "You know, I feel really bad about leaving Kathy." He paused obviously in deep thought. "I regret the fact that I'll never see Jay and BriAnne have their first child … and I'm disappointed that I won't someday have the opportunity to walk Lauren down the aisle."

I could sense his pain and deep regret as he considered the impact that his death would soon have on his family. He loved them all so deeply. He sat quietly, thinking about what he had just shared. And then this glowing smile emerged. His next comment blew me away.

"But I am so looking forward to being with the Lord."

I had known the Lord for so many years, and I firmly believed in heaven, but as I sat there watching Dan at peace, glowing and so excited about his eternal life in the presence of the Lord, the idea moved from my head to deep down in my heart. At that moment, I could practically touch heaven. Both of our hearts were on fire as we then speculated about what it might be like. To this day, it is one of my favorite memories of Dan.

Sadly, not long after, Dan was placed on hospice. The kind and attentive hospice caretakers were a huge support to Kathy, Dan, and the family. They alerted the family that Dan's time with us was quickly coming to a close.

At the same time, Kathy's breast cancer was not resolving with continued treatments. Did we not fully grasp the serious nature of her condition at the time? Again, Kathy tended to focus the family support on Dan. Her selflessness throughout the entire experience became so apparent as we later reflected on these difficult times and how each of us responded to them.

When Dan's last day arrived, the entire family was with him at his home. We gathered around the bed. He laid there motionless with shallow breaths and eyes closed. Each family member took their turn telling Dan how much we loved him, how he had blessed our lives, and how we were going to miss him.

When it was my turn, I leaned over the bed and spoke quietly in his ear. "Dan, you know how much I love you. I have admired you since we were kids. I am so thankful I've had you in my life as my big brother and best friend."

And then, I shared one last thing. Through the years, we had played this verbal game. We would take turns making claims that Mom had taken us aside and confided privately that she really loved us best. Dan was indeed special. This was true in part because he was the first child, but Dan was also an incredibly kind and selfless individual. All three brothers knew well that Mom was so utterly loving and devoted to all her children that she was incapable of favoring one child over another. Just the same, the game went on. Dan and I had worked the routine for years.

So I leaned over Dan and whispered, "One more thing ... Mom really does love me best."

Suddenly he smiled. With that smile, we knew he had heard all the things we had shared as we expressed our love one last time. It was such a great comfort. A few minutes later, he breathed his last.

In the times leading up to this moment, I had worked hard to be the family rock, the one that everyone could lean on. As I looked down on Dan's motionless body, my strength was gone. I had known this moment was coming. I thought I would be prepared. I was not. I went to pieces. I couldn't hold it back. I cried like a baby. We all did. When that moment finally arrives, it is crushing.

Chapter 2

—∽𝔪∽—

BLESSINGS IN THE MIDST OF OUR TRIALS

Over time, as I began to emerge from the pain of these great losses, I reflected on the blessings. During Dan's seven-year journey, I considered all the prayers that had been lifted by so many to our Lord. We had all prayed that Dan would be healed. He was not. The gifts that God had shared, however, and the way he cared for Dan were profound.

While the day in Boston resulted in a diagnosis that neither of us had hoped for, I was thankful for the opportunity to have the expertise of one of the top neurologists in the country. He was knowledgeable, thorough, and so incredibly caring. The fact that I was with this expert at a medical conference shortly after Dan's initial diagnosis struck me as no accident. After receiving his crushing confirmation of the original diagnosis, I was thankful for the ability to be there and support Dan. Our entire family was so loving and supportive as he traveled this difficult road.

Then there was the trip to Indianapolis. We had such a good time on that trip. Throughout that week, Dan was not the poor Lewy body dementia patient. He was just our brother, Dan, wacky and always making us smile. It was a memory that Greg and I will always cherish.

And then there were the hallucinations. While these were clearly another challenge for Dan and the family, the images were never threatening. That is not necessarily the case with Lewy body dementia. The innocence of his hallucinations was yet another mercy.

There was also the fact of his continued intellect, notwithstanding the dementia. Despite his failing memory, Dan was able to think through, analyze, and use notable logic as he evaluated his situations and navigated his way through them. At times, his reflections and analysis of his symptoms seemed like those of a clinician rather than a patient.

Dan also never lost his sense of humor. Dementia patients sometimes change in personality. They often become less communicative as the disease progresses. His memory was crippled, but we never lost the true Dan that we knew and loved.

Each of these was a provision and blessing from God who loves Dan even more than we do. The greatest blessing of all, however, was his new relationship with our Lord Jesus. Dan's faith grew stronger during the nine years that he walked with the Lord than I have seen in folks in their sixties who had accepted Jesus as a child. His spiritual growth was as if he had been shot out of a cannon. The Lord was his focus, joy, and source of his strength. Because of his faith, Dan was able to smile until his final breath.

And then there was that conversation that I will never forget, "I am so looking forward to being with the Lord." Too often we grasp heaven with our head but fail to fully grasp it with our heart. Do we really appreciate the gift we have been given or the steep price paid to achieve it? Dan grasped it. What an amazing blessing for someone who for five decades of his life had relied only on his incredible intellect rather than the one who empowered him with it. In the end, with grace and love, Jesus revealed himself to Dan through the power of his Holy Spirit, reaching Dan through a fellow who decided to bring his Bible to work.

As I reflected on all this, I was becoming increasingly aware of the fact that God sheds so many blessings on us each day. So often they go without notice. We too often focus our attention and energy on our own agendas, personal goals, or perhaps hardships. God's plan was to bring Dan home to himself earlier than we all expected or wanted.

Dan's eternal perspective and my growing appreciation of God's care for Dan made me realize that I need to recognize, appreciate, and thank our Lord for his provisions and love each day, whether during times of plenty or during painful, difficult trials. Chris and I were both learning as we tearfully said goodbye to three family members that we dearly loved.

Chapter 3

—⚬⚬⚬—

MORE FAMILY LOSSES

With Dan's funeral behind us, we still hurt, but it was time to refocus our efforts on Kathy and the kids. It was becoming increasingly evident that Kathy's battle with breast cancer had become overshadowed by Dan's last days. Kathy continued her treatment without complaint, but also without any apparent progress.

I also worried about my mom and dad and how they were holding up with the loss of Dan and Kathy. Any parent's greatest fear is the loss of a child. Each of their children was close to their hearts. They didn't talk much about the loss. I think it was too painful. With periodic visits to check on and support them, I noticed that Dad's breathing was becoming increasingly labored. He had smoked cigarettes since he was a teen. At this point, he was smoking a couple of packs a day.

As children growing up, we never much cared for the smell of the smoke, but we came to accept it as part of our home environment. Dad would periodically switch from cigarettes to a pipe and then back again. As youngsters, it once gave us an opportunity to play a practical joke. One morning, before Dad made his way downstairs, Greg and I quietly snuck down to the living room, removed two cigarettes from his pack, and meticulously emptied the tobacco from the paper shell. We then stuffed the shell with powder from our cap guns. After carefully restuffing the remaining tobacco into the end of the shell, we inserted the cigarettes back into the original pack. We looked at each other with a huge smile. "This is going to be great!"

Later that morning we heard Dad climb down the stairs. There were a few minutes of silence and then the bang. First the cigarette exploded, and then Dad followed suit. He chased us, and the chase did not last long. I needn't describe what came next. It seemed to be such a good idea at the time.

Having been diagnosed with COPD, Dad's breathing had become increasingly more difficult. In the months that followed, there were numerous trips to the ER. Family members would each run to the hospital. The ER staff would typically keep Dad for the day, stabilize him, and then send him home. Unable to quit, Dad continued the habit of sneaking his smokes outside or in the garage. His condition continued to deteriorate to the point where he eventually depended on an oxygen tank and mask to address his worst attacks. It was sad to see.

One Wednesday afternoon, I got a call that Dad was again in the ER. We were concerned, but not overly alarmed. This had occurred so frequently that it was beginning to feel almost routine. I ran to the hospital, as I had so many times before. By the time I arrived, he was struggling a bit but seemed stabilized.

Seeing that the crisis was over, I thought about the trip I had planned that was now only two days away. I was scheduled to fly to Florida with Chris Sutton, my dear friend and senior pastor of our church. We were heading out for a long weekend of golf. A second close friend, Brian Jones, planned to meet us the day after. With Dad in the ER, I was ready to cancel the trip.

The next day, after speaking to his attending physician, I learned that Dad had stabilized and was to be transferred to a physical rehabilitation center. This was an unexpected step in the recovery process. The goal was to work on his physical strength while continuing to monitor his breathing. After speaking to his physician, I got the sense that he was not overly concerned. He suggested that Dad would likely be home within the week. This was comforting news.

While I was convinced that Dad was in good hands and stable, I still struggled with the wisdom of going forward with our trip. After a good deal of waffling, I finally decided to go. I thought Dad would probably be home by the time I got back. With the pain I still felt over the loss of Dan, three days of golf with my good friends might be just the distraction I needed.

We had a midday flight on Friday. As my buddy Chris and I arrived in Jacksonville, I looked out the window of the plane at the bright sunshine. I could already feel the stress starting to melt away. We proceeded to the baggage claim area. With smiles on our faces, we grabbed our bags and clubs and began making our way to the car rental booth. As we were about to approach the counter, my phone rang. It was my younger brother, Greg.

"Hey, Greg. What's happening?"

"Hey, Mike." There was a very long pause. "Mike, Dad passed away last night."

I was stunned. Did I not take the situation seriously enough? He had been to the ER so many times before and had always bounced back. His doctor had not seemed all that concerned. I stood there trying to absorb more bad news. It had only been roughly six months since we had said goodbye to Dan.

I struggled with how to respond. After catching my breath and regaining my composure, I responded, "I'll jump on the next plane home. How are you doing?"

He was clearly shaken. He replied "OK, I guess. Mom and I briefly met with folks at the funeral home this morning."

After Greg and I talked a bit more, I proceeded to the airline ticket counter. The next available flight home was not until the following morning.

I have to say that it was such a blessing having Chris with me at that moment. Chris called Brian and filled him in on what had happened. Next, he arranged to fly back with me the next morning.

Pastor Chris and Shirley Sutton

So we rented a car, left the Jacksonville airport, and drove an hour south to our condo in Palm Coast. After quickly unloading our gear, we jumped in the car again and made our way to a local restaurant for dinner. My mind was still spinning. As we talked, we both found ourselves sharing stories about our growing-up years and dads. Chris knew me well and knew the background with my dad. My relationship with Dad had been complicated. I loved my dad, and I never doubted his love for me. I thought about the many times where he had shown his love in such deep and meaningful ways. He was always there when I needed him.

In my late thirties, I had been released from a senior marketing role with a major pharmaceutical company. This was after over a decade of dedicated service. I had been promoted six times in my last seven years with this organization. Only two years earlier, the senior vice president and department head had told me that I was one of three people at my level that he considered critical to the future of the company. How could this happen? Was it possible that only two years later I was suddenly no longer of value to the company?

Dad at Christmas

By way of some background, the company had gone through several mergers and was struggling. I was considered part of the *old guard*. Countless colleagues of mine had already been let go or demoted. Still, it caught me by surprise. I was hurt and angry.

Shortly after my being let go, I stopped at my parents to share the news. As Dad and I discussed it, he looked me straight in the eyes and said, "Let's take a walk."

I don't remember all he said during that walk, but I do recall one thing that has always stuck with me. He said, "Son, never allow someone else to define you."

It was wise advice. I had learned much from my dad. He taught each of his boys about the importance of having goals, working hard, and being honest. These and so many other things he taught helped shape me. But my dad, while he loved me, could also be quite critical and was known for his temper. Along with my loving memories of Dad are reflections on the emotional and physical pain.

As Chris and I shared stories, I thought to myself, *How fortunate I am to have this very dear friend with me at this moment.* God had provided what I desperately needed at the very moment I needed it.

Early the next morning, Chris and I were on a plane heading for Philadelphia. It was a quiet ride. I sat and thought about my growing-up years. After we landed, I drove to Mom's house, where I met Greg and Mom. They had met again with the funeral director early that morning.

Later in the week, the viewing and funeral were held. Family and friends all came to support our family and pay their respects. This routine was becoming far too familiar. My dad was laid to rest in the local veteran's cemetery where Dan had been buried earlier. I felt washed over, once again, with emotions. I was numb from yet another loss.

Added to my sense of grief was a question that I still do not know the answer to. Dad grew up in the church and attended services weekly with my mom. As his health deteriorated, on several occasions I had attempted to discuss the subject of God's love in an effort to encourage him. My goal was to reassure him that our Lord was walking this path with him. In each case, he would quickly shut me down. Dad never talked about his relationship with the Lord as we were growing up. Was he attending church for Mom's sake? What was his relationship with the Lord like as he breathed his last breath? This sense of uncertainty, along with his death, added to my deep pain.

With our losses still fresh and weighing on us, we all made sure that we, the remaining family, looked for occasions to gather and hold each other close. For the first time, Kathy appeared to be showing wear.

Thanksgiving: Two Months Before Kathy's Passing

One night we all gathered for a holiday meal and some good family fun. There were lots of jokes and stories we had heard so many times before but still made us laugh. For a moment, it almost felt like we were whole again. As I watched Kathy, she was unusually quiet. Was it due to Dan's absence? It had to be so hard. Was it the cancer treatment taking its toll? I watched, not wanting her or the kids to realize that I was. I sat quietly. What might lie ahead?

Not long after, we got a call that Kathy was in the hospital. We were told that she was dealing with treatment complications. Chris and I immediately jumped in the car and headed to Jersey. I left work and arrived first. Chris arrived not long after me. Jay and Lauren were already in the hospital with their mom.

As we walked into Kathy's hospital room, we found her laying there awake, but weak and supported by a ventilator. It was hard to see. We then moved into the waiting area to sit and talk. The kids were clearly shaken. Jay expressed his concerns. Lauren mostly sat quietly. You could see the pain on their faces. I tried to comfort them. Chris had not yet arrived. Jay and Lauren had both been through so much. It had been just over two years since Dan had passed, and we were all still adjusting. Kathy's situation was clearly quite serious, but we all felt it was one she would get through.

She did not. Within twenty-four hours, Kathy had gone home to be with the Lord. It had been only two years since Dan's passing and seven months since we had said goodbye to my dad. As we reflected on her life and her eternal future, we thought about the many years when Dan refused to believe, and Kathy served as the spiritual leader in their home. Her love for the Lord clearly was the foundation for her inner strength and her loving, caring nature. It was a great comfort knowing that she was now in heaven with Dan and our Lord Jesus. Yet it still hurt deeply, with more tears, more sorrow, and another excruciating goodbye. The tidal waves kept crashing over our family. "Lord, please help us."

Kathy

Chris and I did all we could to support and encourage Jay and Lauren, but what do you say? How do you comfort? There were lots of prayers as we clung tightly to our Lord asking that he guide, bless, and comfort these beautiful children and us.

In the years that followed, Chris and I stayed close to Jay and Lauren. We could never fill the shoes of their mom and dad, but we love them dearly and wanted them to know that we will always be there for them.

Chris and I also took on the roles of executor and executrix for two estates during this period. Chris oversaw her parents' estate. I took responsibility for Dan and Kathy's.

Chris spent three to four days each week in New Jersey carefully going through her parents' household. Some items transferred to her siblings, and others moved to an auction house or thrift shop or were simply disposed of. Being the oldest of six children, Chris took the lead while siblings pitched in to help during the early stages. With the busyness of life, the help soon faded, leaving Chris to shoulder the lion's share of the remaining tasks. And then there was the responsibility for wrapping up the financials. It would be roughly a one-year process.

I remained at home in Pennsylvania while handling Dan and Kathy's estate, taking care of our home, tending to our son in high school, and attempting to run the business. As an executrix and executer, the responsibilities that Chris and I carried were great and the work, at times, arduous. We each pushed through as best we could, spending too much time away from each other and carrying the weight of these losses and the resulting duties on our shoulders. It was a challenging time for us both. The stress was taking its toll on us individually and as a couple.

With the passing of Chris's parents, my dad, my brother, and his dear wife, Kathy, I recognized that I now needed to focus on Mom. She was going to need us more than ever. We must be there for her. I pondered what would be next for Mom. I considered her situation and things that might help her through this period.

Mom and Dad had moved to a fifty-five-plus community about six years earlier. She became immediately engaged. Mom played bridge, was in their book club, and served with a group that provided services to residents in need. The latter was her favorite activity. Known for her loving heart, she was perfectly suited for this role. She was often providing a meal or running someone to a doctor's appointment.

Mom had lots of friends. So many in this community simply adored her. I knew that this would be a difficult period for her, but I also knew that her strong faith in the Lord, the love and support of our family, and the backing of her friends would all work together to help her through this.

There was certainly a period of mourning and loss for Mom in the years that followed. Counterbalancing her grief was a growing involvement in her community and its activities. While she seemed to be emerging emotionally, there was also an area of growing concern. Mom was increasingly struggling with basic tasks that had once been quite routine. As a former assistant vice president of a regional bank, she always had a knack for financials. We noticed, however, that she was increasingly asking questions and seeking help on issues that had once been rudimentary. It was not long before I saw the need to take over the financial responsibilities.

Also, when we came to visit, I'd discover little in the way of groceries in her home. One day I went through the pantry, cabinets, refrigerator, and freezer to make an assessment. There were crackers in the pantry and cheese along with a few meal items in the fridge. In all, the supply looked pretty sparse. I did, however, note that there were multiple gallons of ice cream in the freezer. One thing hadn't changed.

"Mom, what are you eating?"

"I don't know. A little this. A little that."

"Mom, I looked in the fridge, and there is hardly anything in there. All I see are cheeses, jellies, and breads. You need normal meals."

Mom just stared at the floor. "I'm fine."

"How would you feel about me arranging a meal service to help you?"

Again, she said, "I'm fine."

Greg and I then decided to take over the shopping duties. Living an hour and a half from her home didn't make this an easy task, but it was one I was ready to embrace.

One by one, the simple tasks were becoming more difficult for Mom. We talked about getting help to assist her with routine tasks in the home. We hired a housekeeper to come once every other week. We suggested other support. She accepted the house cleaning but was uncomfortable having yet another stranger in her home.

As she continued her mental decline, we eventually suggested that she explore the possibility of assisted living. We discussed it periodically but waited patiently, wanting the decision to be hers.

One day I got the call. "Hi, Michael. It's Mom. I've been thinking more about our discussion. I think it may be time for me to consider assisted living."

I was a bit surprised. Whenever we brought it up, she would listen, but we got silence as a response. This was good news. Despite our frequent visits, our current plan clearly seemed to be falling short.

Seeing this as an important step in the right direction but being sensitive to her need to make this big adjustment, I said, "Mom, let's go visit a few that have been recommended. In the end, it will be your choice. Perhaps we can start with some local facilities to keep you close to your friends."

Mom's Birthday

We traveled to various facilities, meeting with their representatives. We took tours in those that seemed more interesting. I also reached out to a friend who was president of a national medical society representing nursing directors in senior care facilities. She lived in southern Jersey and was able to recommend three. It included Pitman Manor, part of the United Methodist Communities network. After a visit, Mom was impressed by what she saw. She sensed that the staff was caring and liked the fact that it was less than five minutes from her current home.

Not long after, she decided to make the move. We promised not to sell her home in case she changed her mind and decided to return.

To be frank, the transition was initially difficult. Shortly after settling in, she had numerous visits from friends who lived nearby. This dissipated quickly as they became busy with life. We did all we could to make her new residence in Pitman Manor feel familiar. We decorated her small apartment with her favorite pieces of furniture and much of her favorite art. She loved her art and had built a beautiful collection. Many of the pieces were from local artists. We did all we could to make it mimic her home. While well cared for, she did miss her friends and her old way of life.

Then came a new friendship with a dear lady named Gwen, a sweet Christian woman with a heart of gold. Smart, kind, and inclusive, she began to invite Mom to various activities. They quickly became best friends. She was such a blessing to Mom and therefore to us. Things seemed to be on the upswing. I thought, *Perhaps this will work out and Mom will be happy.*

Chapter 4

—⁓⁓—

WHY SO MUCH SUFFERING?

A s trials continue to mount, common questions we face relate to *why*. Why am I going through this? Why is there so much suffering? If God truly loves us, why can't God simply make all this suffering go away?

To answer these questions, one must go back to the very beginning. As we read the book of Genesis, we find that God created the world, seas, mountains, sun, sky, and stars. Next, he created man and woman in his own likeness. As God observed his creation, Genesis tells us that he viewed all he had created and saw that "It was good." "Good" for most of us means maybe a B rating or better, but for God, "good" meant it was exactly as he had designed it to be. Our world, as God created it, was beautiful and perfect. Adam and Eve were richly blessed and had all they needed or would ever need. Sadly, it did not last.

> Now the serpent was more crafty than any other beast of the field that the LORD God had made. He said to the woman, "Did God actually say, 'You shall not eat of any tree in the garden'?" And the woman said to the serpent, "We may eat of the fruit of the trees in the garden, but God said, 'You shall not eat of the fruit of the tree that is in the midst of the garden, neither shall you touch it, lest you die.'" But the serpent said to the woman, "You will not surely die. For God knows that when you eat of it your eyes will be opened, and you will be like God, knowing good and evil." (Genesis 3:1–5 ESV)

Appealing to mankind's pride and thirst for more, Adam and Eve were deceived. They bought into the lie.

> So when the woman saw that the tree was good for food, and that it was a delight to the eyes, and that the tree was to be desired to make one wise, she took of its fruit and ate, and she also gave some to her husband who was with her, and he ate. (Genesis 3:6 ESV)

This was just the beginning of a long history of rebellion against God, dislodging his perfect order. One might liken it to throwing stones in a pond. We were all fascinated as children tossing stones in the pond. With each toss, we would watch the circular waves push out from where that stone had struck the water. Equate it to a moment of rebellion in our life or, as it is often referred to, sin.

Think of the man who decides that he likes his administrative assistant more than his wife. This event is like a stone being tossed into the pond. The waves go out as the hurt washes over his wife, children, family, and friends. In the other direction, waves are washing over the administrative assistant and her family and friends. Initially the destruction may have never been thoroughly considered, but it is nonetheless real and substantial.

Next consider the stone as it moves past the surface and begins to go deeper into the pond. We don't see the waves from the surface, but they still exist. These can be likened to the impact of sin over time. We have all heard stories about an abusive parent. Too often we learn that they were abused by their parent, and it can go back several generations. The pattern of sinful, hurtful behavior is not a given. Some choose to break these chains, but it occurs often enough that we must take notice. The stone traveling deep into the water might be thought of as the effect of sin over time.

Now imagine millions of people all throwing their stones into the pond. We have all thrown our stones. Some stones may seem larger than others, but they are all doing damage. "For all have sinned and fall short of the glory of God" (Romans 3:23 ESV).

What have we done to this beautiful, peaceful pond that God had created? This picture is an image of our broken world. The pond is still beautiful by design, just as it was created to be. The stones, however, disrupt and significantly alter that beauty.

We are all living in that brokenness. Sometimes we might ask, "Are we suffering due to the direct consequences of our own behavior?" If that is the case, remember that while the discipline may be painful, the purpose is to correct our path and lead us back to God who loves us. Consequences are not about retaliation. They are about God's desire to forgive and restore us into a right relationship with himself. "My son, do not despise the Lord's discipline or be weary of his reproof, for the Lord reproves him whom he loves, as a father the son in whom he delights" (Proverbs 3:11–12 ESV).

This provides an important clue as to why God does not simply take these consequences away. Our God is a loving and merciful God, but he is also a just God. If there were no consequences, what might our world be like? Would we dive deeper into our sin? Sin, or rebellion against God, by its very nature, causes harm to others. Out of love for us, God desires to protect us and those around us from that harm.

So does this mean that every time we suffer God is disciplining us for our sinful actions, present and/or past? Not at all. Our suffering is very often a result of the broken world all around us. In either case, pain and suffering are inescapable. Our world has become so broken that it is even affecting the natural world around us with such things as our health. As sin prevails, brokenness remains on this earth until Jesus returns. One day sin will at last be eternally removed. Sickness, broken relationships, deception, pain, and sorrow were never part of the original design. Until we are with the Lord in heaven, where death and sin have no place, suffering is and will be an inevitable part of life on this earth.

While still walking the path of this life, there is good news. It is rooted in these essential truths: our Lord loves us deeply, and he is aware of everything in our life that has happened, is happening, and will happen. Because of his deep love for us, he will care for us.

> The steadfast love of the Lord never ceases; his mercies never come to an end; they are new every morning; great is your faithfulness. "The Lord is my portion," says my soul, "therefore I will hope in him." (Lamentations 3:22–24 ESV)

Nothing can separate us from his love.

> For I am sure that neither death nor life, nor angels nor rulers, nor things present nor things to come, nor powers, nor height nor depth, nor anything else in all creation, will be able to separate us from the love of God in Christ Jesus our Lord. (Romans 8:38–39 ESV)

God hears us calling and answers prayers. In answer to our prayers, he may choose to remove our trial. This brings to mind Randall, a former worship pastor from our church. Randall was diagnosed with advanced stage cancer. In love, the church family gathered to pray earnestly for Pastor Randall's healing. In a follow-up appointment with his oncologist, Randall was surprised to learn that this latest test showed the cancer to be completely gone. The oncologist was dumbfounded, unable to explain the sudden and complete reversal. God heard and acted upon the heartfelt prayers. Miracles do still happen.

But what if the trial is not removed? Despite the countless ongoing and earnest prayers for my brother, Dan, he still passed away, just as his neurologist had predicted. Why was Randall healed and not Dan?

We get a clue to the answer in the book of Daniel, as he shares about an event that occurred with three close friends. As we look at the well-known story of Shadrach, Meshach, and Abednego and the fiery furnace, the king of Babylon, Nebuchadnezzar, prepared to burn these three devoted Israelites in the fiery furnace for not bowing in worship to the golden statue of the king. The king challenged the men and our God when he stated, "But if you do not worship, you shall immediately be cast into a burning fiery furnace. And who is the god who will deliver you out of my hands?" (Daniel 3:15 ESV).

Recognizing that God had the ability and power to do the seemingly impossible, they answered, "If this be so, our God whom we serve is able to deliver us from the burning fiery furnace, and he will deliver us out of your hand, O king. But if not, be it known to you, O king, that we will not serve your gods or worship the golden image that you have set up" (Daniel 3:17–18 ESV).

What each man recognized while facing potential death was that our God has the power to deliver us or the ones we love from any fiery trial. His love for us and his plan for our lives, however, is not dependent on that delivery. God's will, whether active or permissive, will be done.

We may have questions concerning the *whys*. We may be struggling in our attempts to find answers. We must remember that his love for us is unconditional. His goal for us is for our eternal future. We may not have all the answers, but will we trust in God and his plan, even if it is painful? As we walk this painful road, what might God be doing in our lives and hearts? How might this impact not only our life but the lives of others? We will look at this topic more closely in chapter 7.

Regarding Dan, Kathy, Chris's parents, and my dad, what I do know is that God's love and provisions remained as our Lord walked that difficult and painful path with us. He did hear and answer our prayers. There were so many provisions and blessings that accompanied the pain and sorrow. The Lord gave us strength when we desperately needed it, as well as emotional healing as we traveled through the grieving process. We were also growing in the certain knowledge that he loves us and is always with us, in the good and troubled times.

When he calls to me, I will answer him; I will be with him in trouble; I will rescue him and honor him (Psalms 91:15 ESV).

The apostle Paul served the Lord faithfully, yet he suffered greatly. He was ridiculed, threatened, beaten, imprisoned, shipwrecked, and left for dead. His reliance on the Lord was expressed in his letter to his dear friends in Philippi.

I know how to be brought low, and I know how to abound. In any and every circumstance, I have learned the secret of facing plenty and hunger, abundance and need. I can do all things through him who strengthens me. (Philippians 4:12–13 ESV)

God never leaves us. There may be pain, sorrow, and more than a few tears. The trial may be removed, or it may not be. Most importantly, we never walk it alone. If we truly seek our Lord Jesus with all our heart, mind, and soul, he will demonstrate his unwavering love for us as he strengthens us, guides us, and brings healing where needed. It may take time and patience, but our Lord never fails us.

Chapter 5

—⟋⟋⟋—

I'LL BE HOME IN AN HOUR

After years of painful losses, it appeared that Chris and I were finally emerging from the long series of difficult trials. Things seemed to be returning to normal. One night, I was sitting in the family room of our home in Doylestown, Pennsylvania, watching an Eagles preseason game. The phone rang. It was my wife. I looked at the clock, which read roughly 7:00 p.m.

She began, "Hi, hon. It's me. I'm at the grocery store and have one more stop to make. I should be home around eight o'clock."

When my dear wife calls and says that she plans to be home at eight o'clock, I know two things: she will eventually return home, and it will not be by eight o'clock.

By nine, Chris had still not returned. The scrubs were now in the game, and I had lost interest. Laying on the couch, I had drifted off to sleep.

Then I heard a voice. "Mike ... Mike ..."

Half-asleep, I began to rouse. My first instinct was that it was Chris, calling me from the garage to help her bring in the groceries.

Then I heard the voice again. "Mike ... MIKE!"

I realized that it was not Chris's voice. I detected panic. I ran to the front door and peered through the screen. It was Beth, our neighbor. Her eyes were wide and full of fear.

"Beth, are you OK?

Out of breath, she responded, "It's Chris. She's been in an accident."

"Where?" I felt my own panic setting in.

"At the end of the drive. Hurry."

I threw open the door and began running down our four-hundred-foot drive. As the scene came into view, I noticed the lights of the police and ambulance. I ran harder. Drawing closer, I saw her. My love, best friend, and life partner, was laying in the street, surrounded by EMTs and police officers.

A female officer quickly approached me. "Are you Mr. Fullmer?"

"Yes."

Attempting to pull me aside, she said, "I need to talk to you."

"First, I need to see my wife" was my immediate and panicked response.

Not letting go, she continued, "Mr. Fullmer, please, I need to talk to you for a minute."

My head was swirling. I saw a second officer behind her. All I could think about was that I needed to see my wife. I pushed the officer back and ran toward Chris. I fell to my hands and knees, crawling until we were face-to-face.

"Hon, are you OK? What happened?"

The scene around me was frantic. An EMT explained that our car had just run over her. Each EMT was busily preparing Chris to be carefully moved onto a stretcher, loaded into the ambulance, and then quickly transported to Abington Hospital, a local trauma center. I looked around me. Everything seemed to be a blur. Hardly able to speak, I just remained by her side. I was desperately trying to regain my composure, wanting somehow to help.

Later I learned the details. Chris had stopped at the end of the drive, as she often does, to get the mail. She, thinking she had put our SUV into park, stepped out and moved toward the mailbox. Suddenly she felt the car moving. The transmission had slipped into reverse. Before she could react, the door hit her and knocked her to the ground while dragging her into the street. As she attempted to roll away, the turned front tires swung in her direction. Before she could escape their path, the left front tire of our Ford Explorer proceeded to run over her pelvic area.

For the next half hour, she laid in the street writhing in pain, calling my name. I never heard her. The distance from our house as well as any neighbor was simply too far. To this day, I picture this scene and think of her crying out my name. It fills my heart with angst and brings tears to my eyes. The method by which she was discovered, I will save for a bit later.

Returning to the scene, I watched as the ambulance pulled away, sirens blaring. I stood in shock. I had experienced various accident-related traumas in my life: a dropped motorcycle, breaking my left collarbone, and a failed ski jump that knocked me out and fractured my right shoulder. Nothing, however, compared to this. I was numb. My mind was foggy, afraid, and confused.

David, our next-door neighbor, took me to the hospital. We were not far behind the ambulance. In transit, I called Pastor Chris. He and his wife, Shirley, arrived shortly after we did. We all had a chance to gather around Chris in the ER as they prepared for her first surgery. I was told that they would need to do immediate surgery to stop the internal bleeding. Dr. Craig, one of the top trauma surgeons in the region, was on call that night. He would be involved in all of Chris's surgeries.

The initial surgery went well. After the surgery, we rejoined her and stayed with her most of the night. Once again, Pastor Chris, along with Shirley, were both such a comfort and blessing. I was also grateful for David running me to the hospital and remaining with me to provide support.

After returning home and catching just a few hours of sleep, I jumped in my car and headed back to the hospital. I arrived at six thirty in the morning. Dr. Craig and the surgical team prepared for her second surgery. This procedure would focus on repairing the broken femur bone in her right leg. After meeting with Dr. Craig, who explained the procedure and what to expect, I headed to the waiting area. I looked for a place to settle for a few hours and noticed a crowd. Trying to focus, I realized it was a large group of friends from church who had come to sit with me and pray. Again, I felt so grateful.

The procedure went as planned. The next steps were a day of recovery and then a third surgery two days later. This final surgery would repair her pelvis, which was broken in four areas.

At six thirty on Sunday morning, I was ready for surgery number three and again sitting with Dr. Craig. He walked me through the plan for this final eight- to ten-hour surgery. He discussed the potential risks and possible outcomes. I asked lots of questions.

"Will she walk again? Will the pain eventually subside? What will the recovery period look like?"

He was encouraging but simultaneously cautious about what was promised. He explained that the surgery would be a long one. Even if all went exactly as planned, there existed the possibility that the hip would break down in the next year or two, requiring a hip replacement. There was also the possibility of nerve damage.

With this, I made my way back to the waiting area. To meet me, once again, was a group of friends and family. The day was long.

After roughly nine hours, Dr. Craig came out to meet me. "The surgery went very well. We were able to repair all the breaks."

I whispered to myself, "Thank you, Lord."

"Someone will be coming out shortly from recovery to take you to see Chris."

For ten more days, Chris remained in the hospital. There were challenges. The pain she was enduring was significant, but Chris, as always, showed her inner strength and proceeded without complaint. Her next step would be spending time in a physical rehabilitation center. Her social worker was busy contacting all the local physical rehab facilities, but without success. After having exhausted all possibilities, she came in and explained that she had arranged for Chris to rehab at a nursing home not far from our home.

This deeply concerned me. Were they equipped to rehabilitate a patient with such severe injuries? I visited the facility and met with the physical therapy staff. They were very kind and seemed committed, but the visit did not allay my concerns. Unfortunately, there did not appear to be alternatives.

Then a couple of days before she was to be released from the hospital, a social worker dropped in to see Chris. She was not assigned to Chris but had heard about her situation and wanted to say hello.

She asked Chris questions about the accident and wanted to know how she was holding up. Next, she asked, "So what is the plan for when you leave here?"

"They have Chris scheduled to go to a nursing care facility near our home," I responded.

She raised her eyebrows. "A nursing home?" She sat for a moment, deep in thought. "I'll be back in a few minutes."

We weren't sure what that meant but waited for her return.

About fifteen minutes later, she reappeared. "I've contacted a friend of mine. She is the admissions director for an excellent physical rehabilitation center about five minutes from here. She said she can get you in, but you'll need to get there in the next half hour to sign the admission papers."

I immediately got the address and headed to the facility. Within an hour, it was all arranged. The facility turned out to be all she told us it would be. The rehab was rigorous but having an impact. The staff was dedicated and very caring. This whole situation was yet another gift from the Lord.

I spent my days with her and remained absent from work for most of that month. Early in the morning, I'd head to the rehab facility to spend the day with Chris. At night, I would head home to respond to calls and emails from friends and family. After a month, we arranged for Chris to return home. My billiards room on the first floor was converted to a bedroom. Everything she needed was brought to the first floor.

She was initially assigned round-the-clock home care. I was able to return to work. The home health aides were reasonably skilled for their tasks, but at times seemed a bit disconnected from the one being cared for. The aides also changed routinely, so there were frequent new faces and new introductions.

One day we received a phone call that they would be sending yet another in a long lineup of health aides. Her name was Natalia, and she would be arriving the next morning.

Natalia arrived, as instructed, and introduced herself. Over the course of the first week, she began sharing more about her background. She was from the Republic of Georgia, northeast of Turkey. She immigrated to the United States during the height of the political and civil unrest in her home country. She had been working as a physician in Georgia but had to give up her profession once she entered the US as its failed to recognize her medical credentials.

Relegated to the role of a nurse's aide, you might think she would be bitter or feeling that this role was well beneath her. She did not. She was hardworking, cared deeply about Chris's welfare, and was, unsurprisingly, insightful about health issues related to Chris's condition.

Her caring heart was, I suspect, what initially led her to the field of medicine. Her love for the Lord and that same caring drive were still quite alive. Natalia was such an encouragement to us both. She became a beloved friend of the family. God had once again blessed us. The pain was still there. The recovery was difficult. Natalia's care and encouragement could not have come at a better time.

Three months after Chris was home, I was scheduled for back surgery to address a disc fragment the size of a quarter. It had been pressing on a major nerve, causing significant sciatic pain that ran down my right leg. The procedure was performed on an outpatient basis, and I was back home that same day. I was quickly back in a position where I could help care for Chris. In the context of everything else that was going on, this surgery was a minor bump in the road. My quick recovery was yet another blessing.

For the first four months that Chris was home, she worked tirelessly through her physical therapy plan. When not in bed or doing her exercises, she was bound to a wheelchair. Over time, she slowly transitioned from a wheelchair to a walker, a cane, and finally to walking without support. The entire recovery period was three years.

As a sidenote, roughly seven months into this three-year recovery period, a valued member of our executive leadership team approached me and asked if I could set aside some time to talk. The company, which God had given me the privilege of starting and overseeing, was now in its sixteenth year. He had been with me a number of those years and was a trusted colleague and leader.

As we met, he explained that another company had reached out and expressed interest in hiring him for a more senior role. "I'm not sure where this might go, but I wanted to alert you. I appreciate how good you have been to me during my years with the company."

This news came as a shock and disappointment. The next logical step for him was my position. At fifty-eight, however, I was not planning on retirement for another four to five years. While I had not yet disclosed to him my intended transition plan, I had already taken steps to begin grooming him for the position.

With the news of his possible departure, I contacted my business partner and good friend, Joe Dennis, in Florida. We talked at length over the next few days. We concluded that it probably made sense for me to make my transition early and offer him the position of president. He was bright, academically accomplished, experienced, and creative. When in group meetings with our medical society partners, it often became clear that he was one of the smartest individuals in the room.

In April. roughly a month after our discussion, I shared with the staff that I would be turning the reigns of leadership over as I announced my replacement and our new president. I could now better focus on supporting Chris wherever needed.

By the end of year three, Chris's recovery had generally plateaued, as predicted. There were still some unresolved effects. There was, for example, damage to the nerve bundle in her left hip. This occurred during the third surgery. Having been warned of this possibility, it was not a complete surprise. It still came as disappointing news. It resulted in drop foot, her inability to fully raise the tip of her left foot. This altered her stride and required her to wear a leg brace for certain activities, like riding a bike. She also was experiencing at least some pain at the end of most days. This was particularly true if she had been overactive.

Chris at the Rehabilitation Center
Later as the "Dancing Queen"

But my love is the Energizer Bunny. She could not be held back. She pushed through the pain and eventually eliminated her daily need for the more powerful pain meds. She even minimized other less threatening medications like gabapentin, a nerve blocker. We now had a new normal, and she was once again quite active. In time, she was even tearing up the dance floor, another praise.

Chapter 6

—⟋m⟍—

PAIN AND ANXIOUS
MOMENTS

As I reflect on God's provision during Chris's accident and recovery, I cannot help but be struck, once again, by the Lord's care. There were so many blessings and provisions. These included:

- Dr. Craig being on call the night of her accident
- David, Pastor Chris, and Shirley being with us that night in the ER
- The friends who showed up at the hospital the next morning
- The second group of friends and family who appeared early on the morning of the third surgery
- The case worker calling in a favor to get Chris placed in a top-rated rehabilitation facility
- Natalia's love and care for us

These were just some of the many blessings during this exceedingly difficult period.

This does not mean that we didn't feel the pain. There were countless challenges. There was the terrible night when the front tire of our large SUV rolled over her body, and the moments that followed while she laid in the street crying out for help with no one responding. As she laid in the road, she was fearful that a car might come through at any time and not see her. There were the three difficult surgeries and ongoing pain while in Abington Hospital. There was a month of rigorous and painful work at the physical rehabilitation center. There were months of rehab once she was home and a three-year period of recovery. There were the resulting health issues that included drop foot syndrome, continued nerve pain, and new physical limits.

For me, a particularly painful thought is knowing that my dear wife had been laying in the street crying out my name while I was asleep on a couch, unaware, too far away to hear her cry for help. There was the uncertainty of her survival. There were countless days where I would see her in great pain knowing there was nothing I could do to remove it except pray. And there are still days when I see her in pain.

Life can have moments of deep physical and emotional pain. In a letter to the believers in Philippi, Paul wrote "do not be anxious about anything, but in everything by prayer and supplication with thanksgiving let your requests be made known to God. And the peace of God, which surpasses all understanding, will guard your hearts and your minds in Christ Jesus" (Philippians 4:6–7 ESV).

This is such an important verse for those who have trusted the Lord Jesus. But does this mean we are never to have an anxious moment? As I consider this question, I think about the account of Jesus in the garden of Gethsemane just prior to his arrest. As the weight of what was about to happen began to press in on him, he spoke to his disciples, "My soul is very sorrowful, even to death; remain here, and watch with me" (Matthew 26:38 ESV).

Jesus knew the horrific death he was about to endure. More importantly, he who had never personally known sin was about to take on the sin of all mankind. He realized he was about to experience separation from his Father for the first time in his eternal existence. The pain and anticipation must have been beyond what we can conceive.

Several years ago, Chris and I visited Israel. Toward the end of our ten-day journey, we went to the garden of Gethsemane in Jerusalem, the very place where Jesus prayed this prayer. As I separated myself from the group and knelt to pray, I quietly tried to imagine what it was like for our Lord Jesus that night.

As I prayed, I was washed over with emotions. The reality of what Jesus endured began to settle in. The feelings seemed overwhelming, yet I am certain that they hardly touched the surface of what our Lord experienced that night. So how did Jesus respond? He acknowledged the emotions. "And going a little farther he fell on his face and prayed, saying, 'My Father, if it be possible, let this cup pass from me;'" (Matthew 26:39 ESV).

Yet his heart was set on the Father's will and moving forward. "nevertheless, not as I will, but as you will" (Matthew 26:39 continued ESV).

Therein, I believe, is the answer. We will have anxious moments. This is a critical time to seek our Lord in prayer. Feel and admit the pain. Ask our questions. We may need to take the time to mourn. That process may take much longer than we want. Ultimately, however, we must move forward while trusting God. We cannot afford to pitch our tent and camp out indefinitely in the anxiety. If we do, our unwavering focus on the pain will distract us from the unwavering love of the Lord. The blessings may go unnoticed. His presence may go unnoticed. In the end, it can only lead us to despair and possible bitterness.

It is not a matter of ignoring it and pretending it does not exist. That will simply prolong the pain. We need to come to grips with the situation along with the pain, clinging to the Lord in the process. This is a time to earnestly seek him, being patient and assured as we walk through it, that we are walking through it together, no matter how long it may take.

In the situation with Chris's accident, I found that some blessings were immediately recognizable. Others were apparent later, upon reflection. Sometime after Chris was admitted to the hospital, I learned of how she was discovered. As mentioned previously, Chris had been laying in the street crying out my name. I heard nothing due to the distance. Our neighbors, likewise, heard nothing. At this moment, however, our neighbor's Border collie began fussing to go outside. It continued whining at the front door. Our neighbor, Cindy (David's wife), stood and opened the back door, providing access to their fenced-in backyard. It is a favorite romping place for their dogs. The dog, however, stopped at the open door, refusing to exit. It instead returned to the front door. Cindy shrugged, returned to the family room, and sat back down in front of the TV.

Not giving up, their dog continued to whine. Again, Cindy stood up and tried to let him out through the back door. Refusing, the dog returned to the front door and once again whined. Finally, relenting, Cindy put a leash on her furry companion and opened the front door. Their dog immediately led her to Chris's side. Cindy quickly dialed 9-1-1 on her cell. Looking toward her house, she noticed our SUV wedged into their front bushes. The car had backed down our drive, pulling Chris with it, entered the street, ran over her, and then did a half-circle returning to our side of the street and Cindy's yard. That dog received some special dog treats the first chance I had.

Moments after Cindy called 9-1-1, our neighbor, Beth, was returning home. As she entered our street, she saw the flashing lights. She stopped, jumped out of the car, and ran up our long drive to get me.

I also learned from Chris, as she recounted her memory of the accident, that shortly before the front tire began running over her midsection, ultimately breaking her pelvic bones, she cried out, "Help me, Jesus." Immediately she felt the tire being lifted from her body. Her pelvis and femur bone were still broken, but the significance of this account became much more meaningful months later.

On a follow-up visit after her surgery and a month of physical rehab, we met with a specialist known as a physiatrist. His goal was to review her rehabilitation progress and determine what additional steps may be needed in her physical therapy and recovery plan.

As he carefully examined her and reviewed her records, he looked at Chris and said, "You know, you are very fortunate that you are alive."

We both shook our heads. I quickly responded, "I know."

He looked at us both seriously. "I don't think you do. You see, with the damage Chris had to her pelvic area, most people don't survive. There is so much vasculature in this area, accident victims typically die of internal bleeding the first night. It is a miracle that Chris is alive. It's also quite amazing that there was no organ damage."

We both looked at each other, stunned.

Chapter 7

———m———

ALL THINGS WORK TOGETHER FOR GOOD

A comforting and familiar verse often associated with life's trials is found in Paul's letter to believers in Rome. The Romans were an oppressive power. It was not easy being a Jesus follower under Roman rule, whether a Roman citizen or the citizen of one of its occupied nations. Yet Paul felt it important for the believers to understand God's watchful eye over each of his beloved children. "And we know that for those who love God all things work together for good, for those who are called according to his purpose" (Romans 8:28 ESV).

This is a profound promise representing God's love and plan for us, but do we really understand it? Let us look at the three major components of this verse. Two we will cover in this chapter; the third is in the next. <u>"And we know that for those who love God</u> all things work together for good, for those who are called according to his purpose" (Romans 8:28 ESV).

So what does it mean when it says, "those who love God"? If you ask the average Christian if they love God, they are likely to respond, "Of course I do" or "Absolutely."

What should that look like? Consider a deep, loving relationship you may have with a parent, sibling, close friend, or spouse. What kinds of things might you work on to enhance or show the genuineness of your love?

❖ Spending quality time together is always a good place to start.

❖ How about growing in our understanding of each other? What makes them tick and helps define who they are?

❖ Then there is inclusion. Do we include them as an integral part of our life in order to strengthen our bond and mutual understanding?

❖ A critical building block is trust. Is our relationship built on mutual trust? Trust is essential to a loving, growing relationship.

❖ Consider serving. If we truly love that person, we will be inclined to show that love through our service to them.

❖ Next, consider appreciation. If we truly love them, we will make a special effort to show them that we appreciate who they are and what they mean to us.

❖ How about selflessness? If we truly love them, we'll want to put their interests before our own.

To be honest, none of us are perfect in these areas, but most will agree that these are the things we want to strive for to strengthen a loving, caring relationship.

So how does all this relate to our relationship with the Lord?

Let's begin with time together. How much time do we spend with the Lord over the course of a day? Do we commit time routinely to spend in his Word and prayer? Life gets busy. We press hard to fit it all in. So what gets sacrificed? Is our Lord at the top of the list or somewhere near the bottom?

Behold, I stand at the door and knock. If anyone hears my voice and opens the door, I will come in to him and eat with him, and he with me. (Revelation 3:20 ESV)

In the time of Jesus, entering someone's home and eating with them suggested close fellowship. The times we spend together with our Lord are incredible opportunities for us to enjoy fellowship and just chat, something commonly referred to as prayer. It's a time to share what's going on in our lives and what's on our heart. None of what we might share surprises our Lord. He knows us better than we know ourselves. It pleases him, however, when we seek him and want to spend time with him because it shows our love. He also wants to answer our prayers with comfort, blessings, and direction, if we are willing to listen.

I love those who love me, and those who seek me diligently find me. (Proverbs 8:17 ESV)

How about time in his Word? These special times also impact our ability to truly know him. Think of God's Word as love letters written by a loving Father to his children. In it, he offers fatherly advice, trustworthy wisdom, expressions of his affection, and parental warnings to keep us from harm. In reading his love letters, we come to know and understand his character, purpose, and deep abiding love for us. The more we read it, the more he reveals himself and the depth of the wisdom contained within. As if this gift is not enough, he also promises to guide us in our understanding of his Word through the work of his Holy Spirit in our minds and hearts.

Your word is a lamp to my feet and a light to my path. (Psalm 119:105 ESV)

Jesus himself made the following promise. "But the Helper, the

Holy Spirit, whom the Father will send in my name, he will teach you all things and bring to your remembrance all that I have said to you" (John 14:26 ESV).

Next consider inclusion. Do we invite the Lord into the everyday moments of our life, or do we compartmentalize our time with him? The tendency, if we are honest, is to have our God time, like church on Sunday and our other times, like work, family, and leisure. But what would our life look like if we invited him into all aspects of our life? As our workday unfolds, do we talk to him? Is he a part of our discussions with our family and friends? Do we thank him for the blessings as they unfold? It might be a quick "Thank you, Lord." Do we ask his advice on day-to-day decisions? Perhaps it is a simple "Lord, please guide me here."

> Then you shall call, and the Lord will answer;
> you shall cry, and he will say, "Here I am". (Isaiah
> 58:9 ESV)

Imagine a marriage where you say, "Hon, eight thirty to five is work time. I'll give you six to seven for dinner. Seven to ten is my time for reading and catching up on my favorite shows. I will check in on you at around ten forty-five before I hit the sack. Oh, I also need to mention that Saturday is my tennis time, and on Sunday after church, it's off to the gym."

One can imagine what that marriage would be like. Are we doing the same with our Lord?

Next, let's next consider service. Do we serve him and put him first? We tend to think of our service to him as volunteer roles at the church. These can be an important way of showing our love for him and others, but what about the rest of the week? At work or in the neighborhood, do we consider our relationship with others as an opportunity to serve him through our love and service to others? Do we think of him as we interact with others? How open are we with others about how God has worked and is working in our lives? How about those who don't yet know him? Do we remain conspicuously silent, or do we share the gift?

> This is how one should regard us, as servants of Christ and stewards of the mysteries of God. (1 Corinthians 4:1 ESV)

What about appreciation? When we pray, do we move quickly to our long list of wants, or do we take time to think about how God has blessed us and thank him in prayer? How often, outside of worship and prayer in church, do we focus on gratitude and appreciation for his love, his daily blessings, and the incredible sacrifice Jesus made for us on the cross?

> Rejoice always, pray without ceasing, give thanks in all circumstances; for this is the will of God in Christ Jesus for you. (1 Thessalonians 5:16–18 ESV)

These are tough questions. Ok, so you are squirming a bit. Again, being honest, we all find we fall short. But this also points us to a huge opportunity. What might our relationship with the Lord look like if we focused on watering these seeds of love? Our love and need for him will grow. Our ability to love others will blossom. We'll have a greater sense of his peace. We'll be armed with godly strength and wisdom. As we strive for a more perfect love with our Lord, our hearts and minds will become more aligned with his. This all sets the stage for the promise found in Romans 8:28.

Now let's look at the second part of this verse. "And we know that for those who love God <u>all things work together for good</u>, for those who are called according to his purpose" (Romans 8:28 ESV).

So what is good? How do we define it? This is an area where many can go astray. Our inclination is for our minds to go immediately to our circumstances. Does good mean my difficult financial situation has been rectified, my health has been restored, the promotion I have worked so hard for was finally delivered, or that my brother, Dan, has been healed? If God cares for our needs, surely he will respond to and fix our circumstances when asked for in prayer, won't he?

First, we must recognize that God clearly does care about our daily needs. Jesus's own words tell us so.

"Consider the lilies, how they grow: they neither toil nor spin, yet I tell you, even Solomon in all his glory was not arrayed like one of these. But if God so clothes the grass, which is alive in the field today, and tomorrow is thrown into the oven, how much more will he clothe you" (Luke 12:27–28 ESV).

"Are not five sparrows sold for two pennies? And not one of them is forgotten before God. Why, even the hairs of your head are all numbered. Fear not; you are of more value than many sparrows." (Luke 12:6–7 ESV).

When Jesus walked this earth, he deeply cared for those he met, whether feeding the five thousand with five loaves and two fish or healing countless people from among the growing crowds. Each day he demonstrated his love for those around him.

On one occasion he visited the home of Simon and Andrew where he encountered Simon's mother-in-law.

> Now Simon's mother-in-law lay ill with a fever, and immediately they told him about her. And he came and took her by the hand and lifted her up, and the fever left her, and she began to serve them. (Mark 1:30-31 ESV)

As was the case with so many other miracles, the word quickly spread throughout the city. The crowd grew desperate for physical, mental, and spiritual healing.

> That evening at sundown they brought to him all who were sick or oppressed by demons. And the whole city was gathered together at the door. And

he healed many who were sick with various diseases, and cast out many demons. (Mark 1:32–34 ESV)

What happened next, however, took his disciples by surprise.

And rising very early in the morning, while it was still dark, he departed and went out to a desolate place, and there he prayed. And Simon and those who were with him searched for him, and they found him and said to him, "Everyone is looking for you." And he said to them, "Let us go on to the next towns, that I may preach there also, for that is why I came out." (Mark 1:35–38 ESV)

Why would Jesus choose to leave for another city when the crowd, desperate for healing, continued to build where he was? It was clear that the suffering of others weighed on his heart. Again and again, he had responded to their needs. While his deep love and compassion for others never failed, were there others, yet to be reached? Had that become his focus at that moment? How important was his teaching that accompanied his healing? Was he turning his focus to the unreached and goals of eternal significance?

God never stops caring about or for our earthly needs in this life. He hears our prayers as we call out to him. He responds with blessings, love, and care

This passage may provide an important clue to help us to better understand God's definition of *good*? How might God bring about good in our lives when our world is crashing in around us? What is God's definition of "good"? This we have begun to touch on but will explore further in the coming chapters.

Chapter 8

—∿—

GOD'S PURPOSE

This brings us to the third component of Romans 8:28. "And we know that for those who love God all things work together for good, **for those who are called according to his purpose**" (Romans 8:28 ESV).

Let us continue to take a closer look at God's purpose for us. If you've walked with the Lord for any period, many of the following verses will seem quite familiar. Please don't gloss over them. Look at them afresh and consider how they might relate to better understanding our life and its purpose, even during the most painful trials.

We know from reading Paul's letter to the Corinthians that of all the things that impact our lives, there are three that are eternal and essential. "So now faith, hope, and love abide, these three; but the greatest of these is love" (1 Corinthians 13:13 ESV).

Love is at the core of who God is. In fact, because of God's love for us, Jesus left his Father's side, came to the earth, and faithfully served his Father and, ultimately, all mankind. Man's response left him ridiculed, tormented, and then crucified. It is that sacrificial act that allows us sinners to be reconciled with our Lord. The result is the incredible promise of a glorious eternal future in his presence surrounded by his love. It all points to love and redemption.

> For God so loved the world, that he gave his only Son, that whoever believes in him should not perish but have eternal life. For God did not send his Son into the world to condemn the world, but in order that the world might be saved through him. (John 3:16–17 ESV)

That piece of his story, if we truly think about it, is hard to wrap our brain around. In John 1:3 we see that Jesus (the Word), along with the Father and the Holy Spirit, played a key role in the creation process.

> [1] In the beginning was the Word, and the Word was with God, and the Word was God. [2] He was in the beginning with God. [3] All things were made through him, and without him was not any thing made that was made. (John 1:1-3 ESV)

Then we, the very ones he created, rebelled against him with our sin. Despite our rebellion, Jesus chose to demonstrate his grace and love for us by offering his own life as a living sacrifice. He took our sin upon himself.

For those willing to give their hearts to Jesus, love him, and accept his incredible gift, our sins—past, present, and future—are thrown into the sea of forgetfulness, never again to be remembered. Being omniscient, or all-knowing, he knew what would be required even before he created us. Do we fully grasp the depth of Jesus's love for us?

As children of a faithful and loving God, love and trust then become our calling in life. When asked by the teachers of the law to identify the greatest of the commandments, Jesus responded,

"You shall love the Lord your God with all your heart and with all your soul and with all your mind. This is the great and first commandment" (Matthew 22:37–38 ESV).

The balance of his response underscores a second calling for our lives. "And a second is like it: You shall love your neighbor as yourself. On these two commandments depend all the Law and the Prophets" (Matthew 22:39–40 ESV).

Clearly God's plan is for us to love him and others with all of our hearts. It is also to embrace and live out the truth, as defined by Jesus's life, shared through God's Holy Word, and revealed through the Holy Spirit.

> If you love me, you will keep my commandments. And I will ask the Father, and he will give you another Helper, to be with you forever, even the Spirit of truth, whom the world cannot receive, because it neither sees him nor knows him. You know him, for he dwells with you and will be in you. (John 14:15–17 ESV)

You are likely shaking your head saying, "Yes, I understand all that. Help me understand it in terms of trials and suffering."

Trials can bring about questions and doubts. While David was a man after God's own heart and had been chosen by God to lead the nation of Israel, his path was not an easy one. When David was leading Israel's battles under King Saul, he would return from battles and re-enter the city of Jerusalem to the chants of the people, "Saul has struck down his thousands, and David his ten thousands" (1 Samuel 18:7 ESV).

David spent years being chased by Saul simply due to Saul's jealousy. Holding on to the promises of God while simultaneously feeling weary and desperate, David cried out to our Lord, "How long, O Lord? Will You forget me forever? How long will You hide Your face from me?" (Psalm 13:1 ESV).

God welcomes our cries to him. He is not afraid of our questions and desperate cries. Despite David's experience with these moments, David also knew that God was with him. "God is our refuge and strength, a very present help in trouble" (Psalms 46:1 ESV).

And even in our darkest moments, God has a plan for our lives that predates our birth. The prophet Jeremiah shared a moment when our loving, all-knowing God spoke to him about his plan for his life. "Before I formed you in the womb I knew you, and before you were born I consecrated you; I appointed you a prophet to the nations" (Jeremiah 1:5 ESV).

In the same way, he has a plan for our lives. "For I know the plans I have for you, declares the Lord, plans for welfare and not for evil, to give you a future and a hope. Then you will call upon me and come and pray to me, and I will hear you" (Jeremiah 29:11–12 ESV).

The challenge is that we do not fully know or understand that plan. In the most difficult trials, it can be difficult to see. The sudden turns in our lives often run contrary to the plan we may have envisioned. "Many are the plans in the mind of a man, but it is the purpose of the Lord that will stand" (Proverbs 19:21 ESV).

God's plan preexisted our birth and is intended to accomplish good with eternal implications. He desires to more closely align our hearts and purposes with his own, and to impact those around us through love and God's truth. "For we are his workmanship, created in Christ Jesus for good works, which God prepared beforehand, that we should walk in them" (Ephesians 2:10 ESV).

When the trials come, our faith gets tested. Working through it, it can become a refining fire.

> In this you rejoice, though now for a little while, if necessary, you have been grieved by various trials, so that the tested genuineness of your faith—more precious than gold that perishes though it is tested by fire—may be found to result in praise and glory

and honor at the revelation of Jesus Christ. (1 Peter
1:6–7 ESV)

Concerned that you are not completely there yet? Not to worry.
None of us are. But are we heading in the right direction? Trials can
make us more God-reliant. Paul had suffered great persecution as
he traveled extensively throughout neighboring nations sharing the
good news of Jesus. In a letter to his friends in Corinth, he shared
lessons learned as he endured these hardships. "Indeed, we felt that
we had received the sentence of death. But that was to make us rely
not on ourselves but on God who raises the dead" (2 Corinthians
1:9 ESV).

As we seek him and lean upon him, our trust (faith) grows.
We learn to seek and depend more heavily upon God for strength,
comfort, and direction. "Even though I walk through the valley of
the shadow of death, I will fear no evil, for you are with me; your
rod and your staff, they comfort me" (Psalm 23:4 ESV).

Ultimately, the plan is to continue to move our hearts into a
closer alignment with our Lord Jesus. "For those whom he foreknew
he also predestined to be conformed to the image of his Son, in order
that he might be the firstborn among many brothers" (Romans
8:29 ESV).

During the period following Chris's accident, we were both
earnestly seeking the Lord in prayer. We are both strong believers
in the power of prayer. Chris and I begin our day with God's Word
and some quiet time spent in conversation (prayer) with our Lord.
To be frank, however, when things are busy and going well, it is easy
to get caught up in our own agendas. Our quiet time can become
shortened and our attention less focused. By contrast, in desperate
times, we tend to focus on our Lord like a laser. It is these times when
Chris and I have grown the most.

I find it interesting that so many of the great people spoken
of in the Bible were people who had experienced difficult, painful
trials. King Saul chased David for years. Paul experienced ongoing

persecution and ultimately died as a martyr. Moses left his position of royalty in Egypt to spend forty years in the desert with a group that bellyached and rebelled. The list goes on and on. Yet God refined the hearts of these individuals as they impacted the countless lives of those around them. The impact continues today. This was often on my mind as Chris and I sought our Lord and walked our difficult path. What is God doing in our lives as we go through this?

Through the trials, God is building character, and character leads to hope. Paul once wrote to his friends in Rome, "Not only that, but we rejoice in our sufferings, knowing that suffering produces endurance, and endurance produces character, and character produces hope, and hope does not put us to shame, because God's love has been poured into our hearts through the Holy Spirit who has been given to us" (Romans 5:3–5 ESV).

Earlier we looked at faith, hope, and love. Hope is built on the foundation of our love for God, love for others, and faith (trust) in our Lord. He is true, faithful, and always loving. God's desire is for these to continue building and shaping our character with a resulting hope in him that is eternal and unshakable.

Trials also offer an opportunity to share what God is teaching us and to be an encouragement to others. During Chris's ten days in the hospital, month in physical rehab, and three-year recovery, friends and family were calling, visiting, and praying while watching her progress. I began posting daily on a website called Caring Bridge. It was a blessing and a wonderful way to keep friends and family informed. It was also therapeutic. For us, it was an opportunity to process and journal our daily experiences, emotions, and lessons learned.

We were also having ongoing telephone, email, and face-to-face conversations with those who loved us and whom we loved in return. Looking back, we came to realize that it was also an ongoing testimony of how God was working in and through us. We did not handle every situation perfectly, but we continued to learn and grow. Over time we were able to reflect on God's countless blessings throughout the painful path we had walked. We had the opportunity to share the blessings and the lessons learned. Friends and family covered the spectrum. Some knew the Lord; others did not. Some were going through a period of blessings. Others were walking through painful trials themselves. All, however, were watching closely.

> Blessed be the God and Father of our Lord Jesus Christ, the Father of mercies and God of all comfort, who comforts us in all our affliction, so that we may be able to comfort those who are in any affliction, with the comfort with which we ourselves are comforted by God. (2 Corinthians 1:3–4 ESV)

So given the choice, would I like for Chris to have never endured this horrible accident? Absolutely. Was it painful both physically and emotionally? Of that you can be sure. While it was not something we would have chosen for our lives, we have both grown from it. Has it impacted others? God only knows how he has and will use it to accomplish his plans in the lives of others. The challenge, of course, concerns our willingness to fully trust in God and submit to his plan. God's eternal promises stand firm. It is our love for the Lord, our trust in him, and our hope found in his promises that we must cling to with all our heart.

Chapter 9

—◊◊◊—

LESSONS FROM THE LIFE OF JOSEPH

As I have sought to better understand trials and God's purpose in them, I've found that the life of Joseph, as described in the book of Genesis, is full of life lessons. Born in the mid-1700s BC, Joseph was the son of Jacob, the grandson of Isaac, and the great-grandson of Abraham, the forefather of the Israelite nation. Jacob loved each of his twelve children but made it clear to everyone that Joseph was his favorite.

Showing overt favoritism toward a child will surely cause all kinds of problems in a family. In this case, an added cultural dimension further complicated the situation. Tradition held that the firstborn child, in this case, Reuben, held a special position in the family. As families, parents, their children, and their children's children all shared the same family plot of land, there arose a particular privilege and responsibility for the one individual who would lead that family group with its multiple generations.

According to Jewish tradition, the firstborn was earmarked and groomed to someday take the place of his father in that role. At the appropriate time, the oldest male would be recognized as the new family head and assume the role as such. The privilege also brought with it a double share of the parent's inheritance. Jacob's unabashed favor for Joseph disrupted the family balance and ran against this well-established tradition.

In this well-known account of Joseph's life, his father chose one day to show his deep affection for Joseph by giving him a special garment. It was long and full, a patchwork of many small pieces of diverse colors, much like that which was worn by the children of nobles. While Joseph was certainly pleased, we can imagine how this gesture fueled the fire of jealousy among Joseph's siblings.

> But when his brothers saw that their father loved him more than all his brothers, they hated him and could not speak peacefully to him. (Genesis 37:4 ESV)

One must wonder about how this favoritism shaped Joseph's view of himself. Was he blind to the overt favoritism his father showed? Had he considered how it impacted his siblings? Was he perhaps feeling entitled?

As we read about vivid dreams Joseph had and shared, we see a message that proved significant as his life story unfolded. How did he handle these dreams?

Now Joseph had a dream, and when he told it to his brothers they hated him even more. He said to them, "Hear this dream that I have dreamed: Behold, we were binding sheaves in the field, and behold, my sheaf arose and stood upright. And behold, your sheaves gathered around it and bowed down to my sheaf." (Genesis 37:5–7 ESV)

The jealousy in his brothers ran hot. What happened next is, again, a story familiar to many. Andrew Lloyd Weber used it as the basis for his highly popular musical, *Joseph and the Amazing Technicolor Dreamcoat.* I cannot help but wonder: has our familiarity with the story resulted in something being lost? Has it now become something like a fairy tale? Are we charmed by the story without digging below its surface to really understand what happened in and through this man? We need to first grasp that Joseph is a real person and a significant historical figure. He set the stage for an emerging nation. Let's continue to carefully look at his life.

Not long after Joseph told of his dreams, his father sent him to check in with his brothers who were out grazing their livestock. They had traveled roughly a sixty-mile journey. He finally reached them in an area known as Dothan. Here, the brothers schemed to put an end to this brother along with his lofty dreams and favored position.

They said to one another, "Here comes this dreamer. Come now, let us kill him and throw him into one of the pits. Then we will say that a fierce animal has devoured him, and we will see what will become of his dreams." (Genesis 37:19–20 ESV)

Not long after, a caravan of Ishmaelites happened by resulting in a new plan. Joseph was quickly sold to the Ishmaelites as a slave. The caravan journeyed on with Joseph in tow. Upon arrival in Egypt,

Joseph was sold to Potiphar, a wealthy, powerful man, and Pharaoh's captain of the guard.

The critical part of the story is what follows. We know that Joseph had grown up under a father who deeply loved the Lord and was committed to following in his ways. While scripture does not provide much information about Joseph's relationship with the Lord prior to this event, we get a hint as we read about his days of slavery. Joseph faced an incredibly painful and unprecedented trial, but the Lord was with him, caring for him and blessing him.

It did not mean that it was easy or that he was about to be rescued from slavery. The trial was to go on, but Joseph was not to walk this difficult trial alone. "The Lord was with Joseph, and he became a successful man, and he was in the house of his Egyptian master" (Genesis 39:2 ESV).

Potiphar saw something different in Joseph. He had also become increasingly aware of the fact that the Lord was with Joseph and was granting him success in the things he undertook. So he decided to place Joseph in charge of his entire household.

> From the time that he made him overseer in his house and over all that he had, the Lord blessed the Egyptian's house for Joseph's sake; the blessing of the Lord was on all that he had, in house and field. (Genesis 39:5 ESV)

As we consider the situation, we must ask ourselves: what would we have done had we been in Joseph's situation? Would we have been filled with anger and bitterness? Would we have played along, doing just enough to stay alive while focusing on an escape plan? Joseph's response to his situation seems to defy the natural human reflex. Don't get me wrong. Did he feel betrayed by his brothers? How could he not? Was he hurting and missing both his home and his father? We can assume that this is the case. Yet he served faithfully, even as a slave.

If we examine Jesus's life on earth, we will find that Jesus provides the perfect example of a servant's heart. How often do we opt for being served rather than serving? Jesus later addressed the subject with his disciples.

"You know that those who are considered rulers of the Gentiles lord it over them, and their great ones exercise authority over them. But it shall not be so among you. But whoever would be great among you must be your servant, and whoever would be first among you must be slave of all. For even the Son of Man came not to be served but to serve, and to give his life as a ransom for many" (Mark 10:42–45 ESV).

What Jesus refers to here is not a literal position as a slave, but rather a willingness to put others first with a servant's heart while keeping our focus on the Lord. Was Joseph now embracing this same lesson? Through all the pain and difficulties that Joseph faced, he clung tightly to the Lord, and the Lord comforted and cared for him.

God blessed his service and brought success to Joseph and Potiphar's entire household. Joseph was still a slave, but Joseph was in the process of learning to serve God through serving others. Joseph was learning to put his trust in God and his plan, even in the most unimaginable of circumstances. There may be times when we feel our world is cracking at the seams. It may lead to pain, confusion, and a desperate desire for relief, but God can do a mighty work in our lives, both in us and through us during these difficult trials. Are our eyes on the Lord? Are we still looking to serve?

The Lord did not remove Joseph's trial, but he did give Joseph the strength to move forward and grow. Through it all, the Lord was building his character, as his hope increasingly depended on God rather than his circumstances.

> Count it all joy, my brothers, when you meet trials of
> various kinds, for you know that the testing of your
> faith produces steadfastness. And let steadfastness

have its full effect, that you may be perfect and complete, lacking in nothing. (James 1:2–4 ESV)

This Joseph was not the same Joseph who danced about as a young man in his multicolored garment, celebrating his dreams about his brothers bowing down to him. Through this refining process, God was moving Joseph in a direction that would ultimately impact countless lives. Yet like each one of us who have put our trust in our Lord, God was still at work, preparing him for God's ultimate plan.

You may say, "Wait. I know this story. I am not about to become the second-most powerful person in Egypt. How am I to relate?"

Perhaps that is true, but how many lives do you touch? How many coworkers, family members, or friends do you encounter over the course of a day, week, or month? Are we seeking, submitting to, and being used by God? Whether we realize it or not, we do impact those around us. Sometimes that impact is greatest during the most difficult trials.

Despite Joseph's faithfulness, he was about to learn another lesson. We sometimes think that if we are faithful, the load will then be lifted? For Joseph, the trials did not end here. Mrs. Potiphar decided to add to his troubles. Seeing that Joseph was "handsome in form and appearance," She schemed to draw him into her clutches, even grabbing his cloak. "Come lie with me," she whispered.

> But he refused and said to his master's wife, "Behold, because of me my master has no concern about anything in the house, and he has put everything that he has in my charge. He is not greater in this house than I am, nor has he kept back anything from me except you, because you are his wife. How then can I do this great wickedness and sin against God?" (Genesis 39:8–9 ESV)

Joseph saw the situation through the eyes of God and fled. Joseph's problems were then compounded when Mrs. Potiphar, unable to draw him in, made false claims against him.

> The Hebrew servant, whom you have brought among us, came in to me to laugh at me. But as soon as I lifted up my voice and cried, he left his garment beside me and fled out of the house."
> (Genesis 39:17–18 ESV)

After hearing her accusation, Potiphar was hot with anger, immediately throwing Joseph into a prison cell. Why would the Lord allow this to happen? Joseph had served Potiphar and the Lord faithfully for eleven years. The Lord was with him and granting him success, yet his situation went from bad to worse.

How often do we place our hope in our circumstances? I have a new job; I'm happy. Twice I've been passed over for a promotion; I'm unhappy. I bought a beautiful new home; I'm happy. The market crashed, and I'm upside down in my mortgage; I'm unhappy. Life is full of ups and downs. We will face hurts and disappointments. Some may be just a struggle. Others are deeply painful. To what are we clinging for hope?

When we suffer, we can run toward the Lord or turn away. If toward him, he uses our suffering as a refining fire. Joseph ran toward him, and Joseph's faith and trust in our Lord continued to grow. Again, we might ask: Does God have a greater purpose in all of this?

> But the Lord was with Joseph and showed him steadfast love and gave him favor in the sight of the keeper of the prison ... The keeper of the prison paid no attention to anything that was in Joseph's charge, because the Lord was with him.

And whatever he did, the Lord made it succeed.
(Genesis 39:21, 23 ESV)

You might say, "The keeper of the prison showed favor to Joseph and placed his trust in him, but he was still in prison. This is a long way from being the favored son living under his dad's umbrella of the love and affection. Again, isn't there a better path to God's plan without all of this?"

For those familiar with the story, we know what comes next. Joseph interprets the dream of a fellow prisoner, Pharaoh's cupbearer. The Lord reveals to Joseph, who in turn shares with the cupbearer that the dream is a message from God. He is about to be released and will return to the service of Pharaoh.

Two years later, when Pharaoh himself is troubled by a dream, he seeks its meaning from his magicians and counselors. When these are unable to interpret the dream, the cupbearer recalls his experience with Joseph. With Pharaoh's permission, he brings Joseph onto the scene where he interprets Pharaoh's dream. There will be seven years of plenty in Egypt followed by seven years of famine. What happened next had to have taken Joseph by surprise.

> And Pharaoh said to his servants, "Can we find a man like this, in whom is the Spirit of God?" Then Pharaoh said to Joseph, "Since God has shown you all this, there is none so discerning and wise as you are. You shall be over my house, and all my people shall order themselves as you command. Only as regards the throne will I be greater than you." And Pharaoh said to Joseph, "See, I have set you over all the land of Egypt." (Genesis 41:38–41 ESV)

From slave to prisoner to second-in-command to Pharaoh, who but God could envision such an outcome? For seven years, Joseph oversaw the production and storage of crops for the coming famine. The famine did come. It gripped the land of Egypt as well as the surrounding lands and their people, including Canaan where Joseph's family resided. It led his family to another divine event, the rediscovery of Joseph.

Again, many are familiar with the story. Jacob sent his sons to Egypt seeking food. When his brothers first arrived, they did not recognize him. It had been more than twenty years since they had last seen Joseph. He was now in his late thirties, dressed in Egyptian garb, his face painted according to Egyptian custom. He stood before them as second-in-command to Pharaoh, and they bowed.

It was a wild turn of events and the fulfillment of his childhood dream. What was Joseph's perspective after these many years of suffering? Did he smile seeing this as justice? What were his brothers thinking when Joseph finally revealed his true identity? Were they fearful? Were they wrought with guilt? Given his power, he could do with them as he pleased. When he finally did reveal his identity, this was how he approached them.

> So Joseph said to his brothers, "Come near to me, please." And they came near. And he said, "I am your brother, Joseph, whom you sold into Egypt. And now do not be distressed or angry with yourselves because you sold me here, for God sent me before you to preserve life. For the famine has been in the land these two years, and there are yet five years in which there will be neither plowing nor harvest. And God sent me before you to preserve for you a remnant on earth, and to keep alive for you many survivors." (Genesis 45:4–7 ESV)

His focus was on caring for the family and delivering God's promises. As an added blessing, Jacob and his sons, with the blessings of Pharaoh, were welcomed by Joseph into the land of Goshen, located in the northeastern portion of Egypt. Sometime later, as his father, Jacob, passed away, Joseph reflected and again consoled his brothers,

> "As for you, you meant evil against me, but God meant it for good, to bring it about that many people should be kept alive, as they are today. So do not fear; I will provide for you and your little ones." Thus he comforted them and spoke kindly to them. (Genesis 50:20–21 ESV)

As we examine Joseph's life, we have a clear illustration of God's plan unfolding in the life of a man who grew in his love and trust in the Lord. He had a servant's heart and was committed to God's will. God used Joseph's life and its circumstances to refine his heart while providing for his chosen people. God continued to deliver his promises going back to Abraham. God had a plan, and it was "good."

By the time the Israelites left Egypt to go to the land promised to their forefathers, it is estimated that their people numbered more than two million men, women, and children. So what does this all mean to us? We may not be destined to become a great ruler or save a future nation from starvation. There is, however, a godly purpose for each one of us, even while we are enduring difficult and painful trials. Oswald Chambers once wrote,

> Perseverance means more than endurance—simply holding on to the end. A saint's life is in the hands of God like a bow and arrow in the hands of an archer. God is aiming at something the saint cannot see, but the Lord continues to stretch and strain, and every once in a while, the saint says, "I can't take anymore." Yet God pays no attention; He goes on stretching until His purpose is in sight, and then he lets the arrow fly.

Reflecting on Joseph's life, what has God called you to? What changes might you see in your growing love for, trust in, and devotion to our Lord? What might God be doing through you in accordance with his special plan for your life? Is God orchestrating something beyond our understanding or even our imagination? Might our trials and our pain be used to refine and prepare us for that plan? How might it all impact the family, friends, and others in our life? Are we ready to march forward, serving and totally trusting in our Lord and our Savior? Following Jesus's death on the cross, he appeared to his disciples and said, "Peace be with you. As the Father has sent me, even so I am sending you" (John 20:21 ESV).

Chapter 10

—⚉—

ROUNDS ONE AND TWO

It was the fall of my fourth year of semi-retirement and roughly one year after Chris had completed her three-year recovery process. A close friend, Frank Sheaffer, visited his dentist for what he thought to be a routine dental visit. As his dentist continued the examination, he noted something troubling. Concerned, he referred Frank to a specialist for additional testing. Not long after, Frank learned that he had developed a malignant tumor in his left jaw. He was quickly scheduled for surgery at Fox Chase Cancer Center in Philadelphia.

Frank and his wife, Carol, are dear friends, and I wanted to be there to support them both. On the day of the surgery, I arrived early to pray with and encourage them both. Frank was calm and smiling. Carol sat quietly. The procedure would involve extracting the tumor, removing the right jawbone, and rebuilding the jaw with sections of bone from the tibia in his lower right leg. Just prior to being moved into the OR, Frank introduced me to his surgical oncologist, Dr. John Ridge. We shook hands. Dr. Ridge was cordial but quite focused on the task at hand.

Little did I know that two weeks later I would be sitting in Dr. Ridge's office as a patient. In a routine visit with my dermatologist, I pointed out a lump in my left cheek. A follow-up biopsy showed that I had developed a malignant tumor in my left jaw area. This, it turns out, was related to a squamous cell skin lesion that had been discovered on my left cheek some time before.

Squamous cell lesions are typically found on the skin's surface and are not uncommon, particularly for those of us who have lighter skin and are of Irish descent. The lesion is typically remedied by dermatological surgeons who conduct a procedure known as Mohs micrographic surgery, or as it is more commonly referred to, a Mohs procedure. During the Mohs procedure, a section of skin containing the squamous cell lesion is surgically removed. This is followed by a close microscopic examination of the area bordering the lesion to ensure that there are no additional squamous cells found. If squamous cells are discovered, another section is cut away and once again examined. This process is repeated until it is determined that the border areas are completely clear. At this point, the area is carefully stitched together and treated with a topical antibiotic ointment to support healing and prevent infections.

Mohs procedures are the standard approach to squamous cell lesions and are conducted on an outpatient basis regularly. They often provide a long-term remedy. Having spent much of my childhood and teen years either at the pool, in outdoor athletic activities, and working shirtless and hatless for my dad in construction, I was no stranger to basal and squamous cell lesions.

Years before, I had experienced a Mohs procedure with a dermatologic surgeon in the area. His procedure, while effective in remedying the lesion, had left a significant scar on my chin. When my dermatologist found this squamous cell lesion, she immediately began arranging an appointment with a local but different dermatological surgeon. He was respected and nearby. All I could think of was that scar on my chin. It had taken years to fade away. I decided that this time, I was going to opt for the help of a plastic surgeon. I could not afford to hurt this pretty face.

The result was surgical recovery with virtually no sign of a scar. That was the good news. The bad news was that he had not completely removed all the pre-cancerous cells. Consequently, I now found myself meeting Dr. Ridge with a significant and sizable malignant tumor in my left jaw area. If not properly addressed, it had the potential of metastasizing and becoming life-threatening.

As I prepared for my surgery at Fox Chase Cancer Center, Dr. Ridge carefully explained the procedure, the concerns, and the risks involved. One of the concerns, he went on to explain, related to the placement of the tumor. My lymph node was wrapped around the tumor, so both needed to be removed. Of equal concern was the proximity of the tumor to the nerve bundle in that cheek. He warned that while he and the team intended to take every step necessary to leave the nerve bundle undisturbed, permanent nerve damage was possible. If it occurred, it could lead to an inability to close my left eye. There also existed the danger of losing muscular control of the left side of my face, causing my face to droop. From Chris's surgery, I fully understood the potential consequences of nerve damage. It weighed on me as I prepared for my surgery.

When the surgery was complete and I awoke in the recovery room after the surgery, the first thing I did was blink my eyes and move my cheeks up and down. Everything was functioning as it should. Thank you, Lord. The procedure was followed by six weeks of radiation therapy. On the last day of radiation, I was walked to a bell in the waiting area where I rang it loudly, signifying the official end of my treatment. Patients around me fully understood the significance and clapped. I was grateful for Dr. Ridge, the excellent team at Fox Chase.

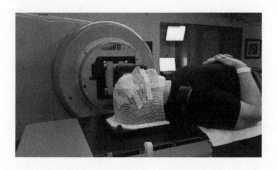

Prepared for My Radiation Therapy

Several months later, after some follow-up tests, I was officially declared to be in remission. I was still feeling a degree of fatigue and had not fully recovered my sense of taste. This is a common consequence of radiation therapy in the facial area. Many items I tasted now had a metallic flavor. I was told that this would likely normalize with time. It did. The important thing was that I was cancer-free. I have now had cancer. Check that box.

Growing stronger with each month, I realized it was time for me to re-engage at work part time. Despite the fatigue, I was needed at the office. The company was struggling. Revenues were declining. The result was the layoff of some key staff that I deeply valued both professionally and personally. The shrinking staff was both troubling and emotionally painful. I needed to get back in the office and help where I could.

In February of the following year, my primary care physician urged me to schedule a time for my routine annual exam. My previous exam had been canceled due to cancer treatments. I was nearly a year overdue. Now on the road to health, it was time for me to get caught up.

Blood tests were normal. Breathing was normal. Blood pressure was my low normal, 110 over 70. Everything looked good. Then as he continued his physical examination he stopped, looked at me, and asked, "Are you aware that you have a fairly significant hernia on your left side?"

Oh goodie, I thought to myself.

He continued, "You really should get this taken care of. I can recommend someone local who's very good."

"OK" was all I could say. While this wasn't a serious condition, it had only been three months since I was told I was in remission. I just wanted a period of health for Chris and myself.

In early April, I had the procedure, and recovery occurred quickly with no major issues. Back surgery, check! Cancer, check! Hernia, check! So this is what getting older is all about. Fun!

Roughly a month later, I began experiencing stomach cramps.

Could it be related to the hernia surgery? More likely, it has something to do with stress. Family losses, Chris's accident and recovery, my back surgery, a bout with cancer, hernia operation, and growing business struggles, I was feeling the stress accumulate. I purchased an over-the-counter oral medication known as a proton pump inhibitor to control my stomach acid. Being a guy, I decided to do what guys do. I self-medicated, ignored it, and waited for it to go away. The pain, however, continued to get worse. I finally decided to schedule an appointment with a gastroenterologist.

In the appointment, I detailed my symptoms and their progression. To provide further diagnostic data, he scheduled me for a CT scan.

Roughly a week after the scan, I had just pulled up in front of my dermatologist's office for a follow-up visit, the first since my treatment for the cancerous tumor. As I pulled into my parking spot, my phone rang. It was my gastroenterologist.

"Mike, it's Dr. Morsbach. We just received the results from the CT scan." There was a pause. "I'm afraid I have bad news."

I know, thinking to myself. *Here it comes. I have an ulcer.*

"Mike, the scan indicates that you appear to have lymphoma. I am very sorry to have to share this news. I have an oncologist I can recommend for follow-up. Just let me know how I can help you."

I sat there silently for a minute, attempting to absorb the news. Finally I thanked him for the call and then sat in the car for another ten minutes just trying to regain my composure. My mind was spinning. I thought I had prepared myself for the worst. I had not. How could this be? I had already checked the cancer box. My appointment with Dr. Toporcer, my dermatologist, was in five minutes. I swallowed hard and proceeded into her office.

I sat in the waiting room, hands folded, wondering what might lie ahead. How would Chris react? How curable was my case of lymphoma? I thought about one my closest friends from high school, Ralph Stablein, who fought lymphoma for years and had recently lost that battle.

Mary Toporcer, MD

"Mr. Fullmer, Dr. Toporcer is ready for you."

I looked up. Back to reality. The nurse walked me to my examining room where I was to wait for the doctor. Over the years, my wife and I had both developed a good relationship with Dr. Toporcer. She is a skilled physician and very compassionate.

She walked into the room. "How are you, Mike?"

"Well, to be honest …" I took a second to gather my thoughts. "I just got a call from Dr. Morsbach. I had been experiencing stomach cramps and thought I was developing an ulcer. He called me to give me the results of my CT scan." I paused and then swallowed hard. "I apparently have lymphoma."

She stood silently by my side. The news had clearly shocked her. What happened next surprised me and amazes me to this day. Dr. Mary Toporcer has developed a strong reputation and is in constant demand. Her waiting room is always packed, and her days are long. After listening to me share my fresh diagnosis, she began making phone calls to physician colleagues asking for input on the best lymphoma doctors in the region. With her patients backing up, she spent well over a half hour making phone calls.

She finally said, "I have got to get back to my patients. I'll continue making calls and will call you tonight with recommendations."

True to her word, she called and offered three names, prioritized. The first on the list was a hematologic oncology specialist from the

University of Pennsylvania named Sunita Nasta, MD. The next morning, I called Dr. Nasta's office to schedule an appointment. Her earliest available date was six weeks out. I was concerned and confused about what to do next. I was anxious to get an appointment with Dr. Nasta. I wanted the best possible clinician on my case, but could my cancer wait for six weeks without serious progression?

Not long after my call, my cell phone rang. It was Dr. Toporcer. "Were you able to get an appointment with Dr. Nasta?"

"She's booked six weeks out," I responded.

"Let me see what I can do. I'll get back to you." With that, she ended the call.

At the same time, Chris was talking to an old friend from high school, Gene Concordia. He had gone through treatment for another type of hematologic cancer and had been treated by this same group at Penn. He too promised to reach out to the group.

While I waited for an update from Dr. Nasta's office, I was referred to Doylestown hospital for a needle biopsy. Four long, narrow needles were carefully injected into my GI tract and guided to my lymph nodes. Their purpose was to obtain lymph tissue samples in order to determine which specific type of lymphoma we were dealing with.

Shortly after the biopsy, I received a message from Dr. Nasta's office. Dr. Toporcer and Gene both got through. In less than a week, I was sitting in front of Dr. Nasta. She would become such a gift, given her highly respected expertise, her caring heart, and her devotion to her patients. Here, again, was another provision from the Lord for which I am so thankful.

During my first visit, after introducing herself, she got right down to business. Looking at the report, she began, "The biopsy results show that you have diffuse large cell type B Non-Hodgkin's lymphoma." Then there was a pause, still looking at the report. Then looking directly at me, she said, "The problem is that we don't know which form of diffuse large cell type B you have."

University of Penn Medicine, Sunita Nasta, MD

I had done a little research before this visit. From my patient portal, I had already read the pathologist's biopsy report. I was aware that my diagnosis was non-Hodgkin's lymphoma. From my own research, I had learned that there were different forms of non-Hodgkin's lymphoma such as follicular and diffuse large cell type B. The pathologist had defined it in his report as the latter. Armed with this information, I looked into the standard treatment for diffuse large cell type B. I found that it typically requires about four hours of chemotherapy, every three weeks, for a total of six to eight cycles. I thought I was well prepared for this meeting, but the news about further subtypes of diffuse large cell type B was new information.

"So what is your sense?" I asked.

Again, looking directly into my eyes, she said, "It appears to be aggressive."

"How aggressive?" I asked.

She hesitated. "It appears to be very aggressive. It started in your clavicle area and has spread throughout your GI tract."

I sat silently absorbing this information looking at the ground. Looking up again, I asked, "So what do you think my prognosis is?"

She hesitated again. "It's difficult to say. Based on the way it has spread, it appears to be stage four, but again, there was an insufficient amount of biopsy material to allow for further assessment. We'll need an additional biopsy to further define the lymphoma."

Gently I pressed. She again repeated the need for an additional biopsy.

Continuing to press, as I sometimes do, I said, "I understand that a more extensive biopsy is needed, but based on what you've seen so far, what's your sense?"

Realizing that I was not about to relent, she reluctantly said, "Maybe fifty-fifty."

I tried to catch my breath. Chris began to cry, and she is not a crier.

Dr. Nasta tried again to explain that it is impossible to give a fair assessment or prognosis without a clearer picture of the subtype, but the words were lost on me. All I heard was "fifty-fifty." One of the things I have come to really appreciate about Dr. Nasta is her careful balance between genuine caring and straightforward honesty. It is what I hope for in any physician, but this message hit me hard.

Next, she said, "I know we are two days away from the Fourth of July, and I don't know what your plans are, but I don't want you going home. I'm sending you across the street to be admitted. You'll begin your chemo tonight. I think it best to begin with a regimen of chemo called R-EPOCH. It will be twenty-four hours a day for five straight days. We will do another biopsy to gather more lymph node material, and then we'll reassess. With this, we will gain a clearer picture of the best next steps. In the meantime, I want to be aggressive in our response."

My head was swirling. I had accepted that I had cancer again and was preparing mentally for chemo treatments, but not this.

From her office, Chris and I took an elevator to the second floor and then a bridge over to the hospital where we checked in at the admissions office. Before long, they escorted us up to my room and got me settled into a gown and my hospital bed. It was all happening so fast. Then came the IV drips. I was on my way. As the evening grew late, I readied myself for sleep. My mind was still spinning. I began to think through the things I needed to take care of if the 50 percent went the wrong way. In time, the exhaustion overtook me, and I drifted off to sleep

The next morning, I had visitors. Ken and Lynn Kirkner have been dear friends of ours for some time. I was happy to see them and encouraged by their presence, but my mind was fixated on the potential implications of my death. It wasn't as much my fear of death as it was a feeling of being overwhelmed and sensing a desperate need to prepare for it, if indeed it was coming.

Ken looked at me, concerned. "So how are you holding up, Mike?"

I related the story of my visit with Dr. Nasta the day before, including the possible prognosis. This clearly caught them both by surprise. They understood why I was here in the hospital, but neither had any idea about the stage of my cancer or the potential prognosis. Both put on their best face to keep me encouraged.

"If I'm dying," I continued, "there are a number of things I need to get in order. I have a binder that has all our information on insurance policies and key contacts. I'll need to go through and update that."

I laid in my hospital bed deep in thought. "And if I'm dying," I continued, "I'll also need to print out Quicken reports for Chris, so she has a clear sense of our financials. She'll never be able to navigate the online financial reports."

I could see Ken starting to squirm in his seat. He had obviously not come prepared for this conversation.

"I'll need to figure out how I'm going to break this to my brother, Greg, and my brother's children, Jay and Lauren. Jay and Lauren have all already been through so much with Dan and Kathy's passing. How am I going to break this news to them?"

Ken looked at Lynn, clearly shaken by this conversation. She just sat and listened intently.

I had been going on with my "if I'm dying" speech for roughly a half hour when Ken said, "Lynn, we should probably get going and let Mike get some rest."

As I looked at Ken, I finally realized what I had just put him through. They did eventually get up to leave, promising to lift us up in prayer. I thanked them and laid there in my hospital bed thinking about what I had just done. I needed to be more aware of how this was affecting those around me.

Chris arrived shortly after they left. She came ready to stay with me well into the evening. I related what had occurred and my regrets over how I handled it. Chris sat and listened. She spent the day doing what she could to comfort me and provide a distraction from this bombshell that had just been dropped on us both.

That night, as I prepared for a night of sleep, I bowed my head and prayed with all my heart. "Lord, if you are getting ready to take me home, help me to accept and embrace it. Please give me your peace, Lord. Please take care of Chris and our children, Jenn and Tim. Finally, Lord, please help me to finish strong. With the time that I have left, whatever that may be, please use me to somehow serve you. It is in your precious name, Lord Jesus, that I pray. Amen."

It was a simple prayer. The response, however, made me realize that it was perhaps one of the most powerful prayers I had ever prayed. As I prayed, everything and everyone around me momentarily disappeared. It was just me, seeking my Lord with every fiber of my being.

His response was beyond my expectations. I awoke the next morning and felt total calm, a deep calm and peace like I've never experienced in my entire life. God was with me, and I was okay. No, so much better than okay. It is difficult to explain. I was still hooked up to the chemo drip. I was still laying in a hospital bed. My prognosis was the same as the day before. Yet I had peace. I felt a deep sense of total peace and God's presence with me.

During that week, I met so many folks in that hospital. With round-the-clock care, I was meeting physicians, nurses, and aides from all three shifts. I also met numerous patients as I walked the hallways, with my IV pole in tow. Some patients walked the floors simply to break the monotony of the long days in a hospital room.

With nowhere to go and lots of time to get there, I decided to engage. I came to realize that there were two major groups of people on this hospital floor. First, there were the patients, each attempting to come to terms with their serious illness, trying to stay strong, and fighting back fear, confusion, and despair. The second were the healthcare providers. These dedicated professionals were trying desperately to save lives, destroy the cancer, and offer hope to their physically and emotionally fragile patients. Both groups needed encouragement. That, I decided, would be my charge while I was here.

I chatted with staff members whenever I could. "How long have you been working at Penn? Are you originally from this area? What prompted you to choose a career in healthcare? Do you enjoy it? Any interesting hobbies?"

For patients, I'd first introduce myself. "How long have you been in the hospital? Do you live nearby? How are you holding up? Are you loving the food like I am? It is just awful."

Over the course of the week, these "getting to know you" discussions began to run deeper. Throughout the week, God opened countless doors, allowing us to discuss deeper spiritual issues. It was amazing. I found so many of these conversations to be Spirit-led.

I also went back to posting updates on Caring Bridge. The list of followers was growing. It included family, friends from church, friends from the neighborhood, and longtime friends going back to my high school years.

As the week ended, I signed the discharge papers, met with social services to discuss follow-up, and began gathering my things for the trip home. I readied myself for discharge when the attending physician stopped by to let me know that the second biopsy results were finally in. They had determined the subtype I had was one of the more common and treatable subtypes. With this, my prognosis improved significantly. Follow-up would involve visits to an outpatient cancer treatment center rather than hospitalization. I was scheduled for five more cycles of chemo known as RCHOP, each lasting three to four hours. At the end of this period, they would reassess.

This was great news. Chris and I walked around the floor thanking those who had been involved in my care and went out on a high note. Thank you, Lord. Thank you for this good news. Thank you for this caring and very capable team that treated me. Thank you for the peace you provided. Thank you for the opportunity to share with others what you mean to me.

Once home, we had in-home regular nursing care for the purpose of monitoring my progress and maintaining my IV port. The visiting nurses were attentive and kind. I was weak, and my activities were limited in the beginning, but I was home and thrilled to be there.

My treatments continued as planned. Every three weeks, I was back for another outpatient chemo session. My hair had fallen out, but ironically my mustache remained. I had lost over forty pounds. I was becoming increasingly weak, but each treatment was taking me one step closer to the finish line.

After my fifth outpatient chemo session, sixth treatment overall, I was told that my treatments were complete. Again, it was another walk to the bell, a quick ring, and applause. I made it.

A few months later, as we approached Christmas, I underwent another PET scan. Hopeful but a bit apprehensive, I waited for the results. As Dr. Nasta entered the exam room, I noticed that she had this pleased look on her face. "Mike, the PET scan results are in. You are in full remission."

I sat back in my chair and relaxed. Chris and I both smiled at each other. Again, thank you, Lord. Cancer bout number two. Check that box.

Dr. Nasta then went on to explain the follow-up plan: periodic return visits for blood tests and scans to ensure the cancer had not returned. With this good news, Chris and I proceeded to a local restaurant a short walk from Penn's Perelman Center. It was a local spot we had come to appreciate. Next would be calls to family and some close friends, and then an update on Caring Bridge. This was such an important milestone. Again, thank you, Jesus.

While still weak and easily fatigued, it wasn't long before I was back reengaging at the company. The company was continuing to struggle. Over the next nine months, I thought it best to increase my involvement to two days per week. My successor remained in charge while I focused on financial issues and strategic and tactical assessment. I noted that many of the processes and procedures that had been in place during my fifteen-plus years of leading the company were changing. We were also experiencing cash flow issues. An even greater concern related to medical society partnerships that I had personally been involved in building over the past two decades. Many were slowly disappearing. I was growing increasingly concerned. I realized I needed to refocus in some areas and address financial issues requiring immediate attention.

Chapter 11

———————

THREE'S A CHARM?

With the ringing in of the new year, I looked forward to a period of health and normalcy. I was still in the process of regaining my strength and energy but was feeling optimistic. On the morning of January 4th, the phone rang. I looked at the caller ID. It was my younger brother, Greg. I hadn't seen or spoken to him since Christmas day.

"Hey, Greg, what's happening? Happy ..." Suddenly there was uncontrollable sobbing at the other end. "Greg?"

His muffled response was "It's me."

I could barely make out what he was saying. "Are you OK?" I had not heard Greg in tears since we were children.

"It's Sue," he sobbed.

"What about Sue?" I asked quickly.

There was a period of no response with more sobbing. "She's dead!"

"She's what?" I could not believe my ears.

"She's dead. I tried to save her, but I couldn't." After another pause, then Greg continued, "I couldn't save her." He began crying uncontrollably again.

Through the sobs, he explained that she got up that morning

feeling poorly. He sat with her on the living room couch, concerned and committed to staying with her until he could figure out how best to help her. After a period, she insisted that she was beginning to feel better. After sitting with her for a bit longer, she assured him that it was passing. Greg jumped into the shower to get ready for work. While in the shower, he heard a crash. Rushing into the living room, he found Sue laying on the floor. She had suffered a massive heart attack. There had been no previous signs or symptoms.

Greg and Sue

"I tried to save her, but I couldn't. I couldn't save her." The cries were growing stronger. "I don't know CPR. I couldn't save her," he kept repeating.

I sat and listened as he continued to cry. We all loved Sue dearly. "Lord, help us, please," I prayed silently. I tried to console Greg. What do you say, except "I love you" and "I will be here for you"? My heart was wrenching.

So we planned yet another funeral. There were so many friends and family that we kept gathering for this one reason. I made up my mind that I would be there for Greg. With my trips each week to Jersey to see Mom in the nursing home, Greg and I got together for frequent lunches and to catch up. He was broken. They did everything together. Sue was such an integral part of his life.

With Sue's passing, I could not help but reflect on an earlier trip we had taken to Lancaster, Pennsylvania. It was the three brothers and our wives. Lancaster is home to a large base of Amish families with their simple dress, horse-drawn carriages, and deep religious convictions. The beautiful countryside, kind people, and small local shops make it a favorite destination for many in the area. Our weekend together was full of delicious dining, laughter, and good fun. It is, to this day, one of my favorite adventures together.

As I looked at the photo from that weekend, with the six of us in front of our hotel, it is hard to believe that three of the six are no longer with us, my loving bride had been run over by our car, I was in the process of recovering from my second bout of cancer, and my brother, Greg, was dealing daily with the painful loss of his dear wife and the love of his life.

The Brothers and Our Wives

As January continued to unfold, I felt my health beginning to grow stronger. In the previous month, my buddy, Frank Sheaffer, told me about a program for cancer survivors called *Thrive* being offered at the local YMCA. He had just completed their four-month program. He shared how much it had impacted him. It provided an opportunity to gain exposure to the various programs offered by the Y and participate in a personalized workout program to regain strength. It also gave me an opportunity to gather with fellow cancer survivors who had firsthand insights into the difficult journey with cancer.

While I tried to be reasonably active during my treatments to maintain my strength, chemo is hard on the body. A breakdown in strength and agility happens relatively quickly. I was thrilled to have this opportunity to rebuild, and I deeply appreciated this no-fee service being offered at our local Y.

The instructors were caring and knowledgeable. It didn't take long for each individual on our eight-member team to get into their respective routine. Anxious to rebound quickly, I pushed myself hard and saw progress. Along the way, we transitioned from being a team to a group of friends. Five years later, we still meet for dinner every four to six months to stay in touch.

With the completion of the Thrive program, I wanted to continue to build upon my work to date. Chris and I joined the YMCA as a family. With this, I continued and expanded my weekly workout routine.

One day, as I finished my shoulder presses, I noticed a lump in the bicep area of my right arm. *Wonderful,* I thought to myself. *I've pulled something.*

Being a guy, I once again did what guys do. Yes, I'm a slow learner. I ignored it and waited for it to go away. It did not. I eventually contacted a local orthopedic specialist and arranged an appointment.

The specialist was knowledgeable and thorough. After a careful exam, he explained, "It's probably just a hematoma." A hematoma refers to swelling due to blood clotting, in this case just under the skin in my right bicep area. It can at times be caused by an excessive strain.

Knowing my inclinations, I thought, *That seems reasonable.*

"Just the same," he continued, "given your history, it's best to follow up with a CT scan."

A week later, he called to share the results. "Mr. Fullmer, I am sorry to have to tell you this." There was a brief pause, and then he continued, "It appears that the lymphoma is back."

I was stunned. This led to another PET scan. A week later, I was back in Dr. Nasta's office at the University of Penn. I went to my patient portal just prior to the visit and read the radiologist's report.

Dr. Nasta gave me a warm welcome but showed clear signs of concern. "The PET scan shows a mass emerging from your right bicep area," she explained. "I had the radiologist go back to review the PET scan taken back in December."

This had been done just prior to my being declared in remission. She explained that apparently the image did show a hot spot in the area of my right bicep. With PET scans, radiologists look for hot spots as well as masses to indicate a potential tumor. In this case, the radiologist saw the hot spot but saw no mass. Since a mass was not apparent, and knowing I was involved in a rigorous workout routine at the gym, the radiologist assumed the hot spot was the result of inflammation from a muscle strain. The mass, it turned out, had been hidden since it was wedged between the bicep muscles.

This was both good and bad news. The good news was that I was not experiencing a relapse and the cancer had not spread to other parts of my body. I also realized that had it not been for the workouts, which ultimately exposed the tumor, I might have gone a long period without detection. This, in turn, might have allowed the tumor to metastasize and spread elsewhere in the body. The bad news was that I was about to go back into treatment, once again, with an even more rigorous regimen.

"The treatment at this stage," Dr. Nasta continued, "will be a stem cell replacement."

If it were not happening to me, it would have been a fascinating learning experience. I was to receive an autologous stem cell transplant. Translated, it meant that the stem cells would come from me as the patient rather than from an outside donor. This, when possible, eliminates many of the potential complications of rejection.

The first step in a stem cell transplant is to inject a drug into the bone marrow, which causes stem cells, the building blocks of our immune system, to move from the bone marrow into the bloodstream. In step two, the blood is extracted from the patient and run through a machine that spins and extracts the stem cells from the blood. This same machine then returns the blood to the patient's body. For step three, the patient is hospitalized, put in isolation, and given massive doses of chemotherapy to kill any remaining cancer cells. After roughly a week, the chemo will have also virtually killed the patient's immune system. At this point, the stem cells are reinserted into the blood to rebuild the immune system. The entire hospitalization lasts roughly a month.

Being in the hospital for almost a month is a difficult experience to explain. Once again, I bowed my head and earnestly sought the Lord. I prayed a similar prayer to the one I had prayed in the hospital after my first diagnosis. I prayed I would be able to accept my situation regardless of the outcome. I prayed that God would care for my family. I prayed for peace. "Lord, please give me peace." Lastly, I prayed that God would use me.

Once again, the Lord delivered in a big way. To be clear, this does not mean that I moved forward without a concern or an anxious moment. What it did mean was that God's presence walked with me through every step, granting me incredible peace despite my circumstances.

This would be unlike my previous hospitalization. Because of my vulnerability to infections with a now compromised immune system, I would not be encountering other patients. So I focused on encouraging my contacts within the healthcare team. Chris had brought me reading materials and purchased colored pencils and a drawing pad so I could sketch. This was such a passion of mine growing up. I often talked to Chris about someday returning to this passion.

The first night I was given my initial dose of chemo.

"Mike, the initial dose has an alcohol base," Dr. Nasta explained, "so you may feel some effect."

As the night wore on, my mind fogged. I stumbled on my words and felt like the fraternity brother who should not have chugged that last bottle of beer. I pushed the nurse's button at my bed.

A few minutes later, she arrived. Looking concerned, she asked, "Are you okay, Mr. Fullmer?"

Attempting to gather my thoughts, I responded, "Hi. I was told that I might feel some effect from this initial treatment. I must say I'm higher than a kite."

She just smiled. "The chemo regimen you just received can have that effect. Is there anything I can do for you?"

I shook my head no and slouched down in the bed. This was an interesting start. The treatments that followed were tough. I had the good fortune of not experiencing nausea and vomiting during my previous treatment series a year earlier. That good fortune came to an end. For a few days, I hugged the rubber tub they had provided like a dear friend. In time, the chemo ended, the side effects passed, and I laid in my bed completely wrung out.

The next step was the reintroduction of my stem cells. With this, I was on the road to rebuilding my immune system and recovering from the effects of the chemo. As I grew stronger, I began to reengage with the staff. By now, I had been there two weeks, and I was becoming increasingly familiar with those charged with my care. Like my previous hospital experience, our conversations often moved from "getting to know you" discussions to the deeper issues of life.

One conversation I had made a particularly strong impression. One afternoon, a young medical student knocked on my door. Not wanting to use her real name, let us call her Angela.

With a warm smile, she introduced herself. "Hi, my name is Angela. Sorry to bother you, but I'm taking a course that looks at the impact of one's faith on health and well-being. Someone had suggested that I talk to you. Would that be OK?"

I smiled. "Not much happening here. I'd be happy to talk."

She looked at me and paused. "You seem awful happy for someone who's going through what you are."

"I won't kid you. I've had more fun than this. But God is good even in the difficult situations." After talking for a while, I asked Angela, "If you don't mind, let me ask you a question. What do you think about the question you posed, and how would you describe your relationship with the Lord?"

She began by talking about her growing-up years. "I grew up in the church but can't say that I go much anymore. My mom says that each person has to decide who God is and what that relationship is supposed to look like."

I smiled, and from that, we moved into a discussion about the search for truth and God's Word. I shared my experience of over thirty years of reading and studying the Bible and the impact it has had on me. I talked about my desire to better understand the truth about who I am, who God is, and the impact the Bible has had in answering those questions.

Then we moved on to discuss what it means to have a personal relationship with our loving Lord, the meaning of God's grace, and the power and work of the Holy Spirit. We must have talked for almost an hour. Before I had a chance to ask if she had ever made a personal decision to invite Jesus into her life, she looked at her watch, announced that she had to run, and scurried out the door.

Over the next few days, I asked to meet with one of the hospital's chaplains I had met earlier. I hoped to make a plea for her to follow up with Angela. Unfortunately, the chaplain was away on vacation and would not be returning for another two weeks. So I handed a note to a member of the staff who promised to pass it on upon her return.

Almost a week later, I heard a knock on the door. There stood Angela with two colleagues.

"Mr. Fullmer, hello, it's me again. I brought a couple of friends. Would it be OK if we talked again?"

Welcoming them in, we reengaged. We began revisiting some

of the same topics. As we finished, we all thanked each other for the time together. I never saw Angela again, but I often wonder about who God may have placed in her life next. I've considered what a joy it was to see God's Holy Spirit at work and being allowed to be a part of the experience.

As children of the promise, saved by the blood of Jesus Christ, and through his incredible grace and love for us, we are called to share what we have learned and been blessed to experience. I have come to realize it is God's love shining through us that engages. His Holy Spirit is working in the hearts and minds of both the one sharing and the one listening. This is what changes hearts. I am a reasonably competent communicator, but so many times I have seen something that occurred in these conversations that was far beyond me. It is God who saves, but he gives us the privilege of being a part of what he is doing. These moments are special. Each conversation with Angela was clearly one of those moments.

Spending countless hours in my room waiting for the day of my discharge, I wrote prolifically and almost daily in Caring Bridge. I shared from my heart my experiences and things that God was teaching me. Throughout my time in the hospital, I was so thankful for having Chris at my side. Chris was a constant encouragement.

Finally the day came when they walked into my room to review my discharge papers. It was such a happy day. We exited the hospital, me in a wheelchair and Chris right behind me. There stood our car, engine running, waiting to take me home. I will be so happy to eat real food again. Lord, thank you for being the source of my strength and peace through it all.

Chapter 12

—~m—

TRUST

O ver the months that followed, I visited the University of Penn's outpatient facility in Berwyn, Pennsylvania, for a series of radiation treatments. By the fall, my cancer therapy was finished. My latest PET scan had shown that my body was clear of non-Hodgkin's lymphoma. I once again rang the bell. It was time to begin pouring myself back into the company.

I returned to the company, this time engaging as an employee, working three days per week. We were now in our twenty-second year of business. After five years, my formal retirement was officially over. Not long before, the company had experienced a second round of layoffs. The downward trend was continuing, and I needed to help wherever I could. One day I was in looking for my replacement and saw that his light was out. I poked my head into the office next to mine and asked Jen if she had seen him. Jen was an experienced member of our Project Services (operations) staff. She had been with the company for many years.

She shook her head no and stared at me in silence.

I waited, looking back. "Jen, are you OK?" I could tell she wanted to respond but was struggling with whether to and what to say. Closing the door, I asked, "What's going on? Are you OK?"

Again, she sat there wrestling with her thoughts. Finally, she began to share her deep concerns about the company's focus and current path. In conversations with others, I learned that Jen was not alone in these concerns. Not long after this, Jen submitted her resignation and moved on to a new opportunity.

In my discussions with others, I learned that the company was spending an increasing amount of time on a newly launched initiative. The initiative was innovative and garnered a great deal of interest from our colleagues in the field of medical education. It was often a topic of discussion at our annual industry conference. Unfortunately, while we were excited about breaking new ground, there were problems. We were showing significant profit losses on the projects associated with the initiative. The revised focus was also impacting our services in other areas. We were losing ground on initiatives tied to our long-standing medical society partnerships. Many of these relationships went back ten to twenty years and played a key role in our success in serving physicians, nurses, NPs, PAs, and pharmacists. Our role was to update clinicians on the latest developments, treatment strategies, and clinical data, all with the goal of improving patient outcomes.

The new initiative consumed much of our new leader's time as he filled the role of planner, coordinator, and collaborator with a key oncology society partner. He was fully engaged in its planning and implementation. The time that he spent focused on the initiative, combined with his associated increase in travel, lessened his availability in all other areas.

I met with him, sharing the concerns as well as thoughts on possible strategies to address them. He listened patiently but offered little in the way of a response. He then shared his growing concern with my reengagement in the company and the confusion it might cause relative to our respective roles of leadership.

Sensitive to his concerns, but simultaneously recognizing the need for a turnaround in our current trends, I routinely sought God's wisdom through prayer. I asked for direction on how best to navigate this situation. For the first time in over twenty years, I was having concerns about the future viability of the company. The company had grown and been so blessed. After years of investment and hard work by all concerned, it was difficult to watch and accept the position we were in. I continued doing everything I could to rebuild and strengthen the company.

Despite my efforts and the efforts of those around me, the downward trend continued. I continued praying prayers that went something like this, "Lord, I realize that this was, is, and always will be your company, not mine. I have had the privilege of starting and serving you in this company. I've tried to do my best to care for the company and the special staff you've entrusted to me. If it is your decision to bring it all to a close, please help me to accept it. If there are things I need to do to help us turn the corner, help me to see and do them. Please give me peace and the ability to accept your will, whatever that may bring. I pray this in your holy name, Lord Jesus. Amen."

There were encouraging moments that followed and positive changes that occurred, but the overall trend remained troubling. I stressed and strained. I pushed even harder to reverse our current direction. I felt no peace. I would often lie awake in the middle of the night with my mind spinning over things I might do next. I considered new initiatives and platforms. I stepped up efforts to create and support new initiatives. Some were already in process and had proven profitable and appreciated by our healthcare audience. We began setting specific tactical goals and deadlines related to our plans. We scheduled periodic update sessions to track and discuss our progress. I was involved in ongoing discussions with new potential medical society partners. With our existing society partners, I worked at reestablishing initiatives that had been successful but had faded away.

As both our revenues and staff continued to shrink and having not resolved our new leader's growing concern with my continued involvement, we both ultimately came to the same conclusion. It was probably best to part ways. So I once again took over the reins of leadership resuming the full-time position as president and CEO. I was determined to dive in fully. I was ready to do whatever was needed to turn this thing around.

Shortly after, we were hit with yet another major bombshell. I learned that a key member of our leadership team, Kristen, would be leaving us. As Director of Medical Education, Kristen was appreciated by all as a solid leader, major contributor, and valued member of our corporate family. Kristen shared with me that colleagues from an earlier employer had pulled together and launched a start-up in the field. With its increasing growth, they needed leadership in her areas of strength. They offered Kristen a more senior position.

Unfortunately, it was a role in which I already had a successful executive leader, one who I highly valued and had been with me for over twenty years. Kristen's new company had also offered her a major bump in salary and an equity position in the start-up. Having recently married and purchased a new home, I can only imagine the concerns she must have had regarding our revenue trends. It had to have contributed to her decision.

I engaged Kristen in a discussion regarding a counteroffer. I found myself unable to engage her with a sufficient counter. With over 50 percent of the company's revenues tied specifically to Kristen's efforts, this hit me hard. But simultaneously I recognized that this new position was a great opportunity for Kristen. Having failed in my efforts to retain her, I focused on congratulating her and supporting her in her transition. I told her how much we would all miss her. The staff and I all joined together for a celebratory send-off event. It was not lost on anyone, however, what this meant to the company.

Again, I turned to prayer. I prayed a similar version of the prayer mentioned previously. I thought about the peace that followed my prayers after each cancer diagnosis. It was so profound. Despite ongoing prayer over this issue, there was no peace. I pushed myself harder and wrestled mentally with what to do next. I had more sleep-deprived nights.

We continued seeing improvements and encouraging signs, but the problems ran deep. Within a couple of months of Kristen's departure, we had found a replacement. Sadly, this individual struggled and fell woefully short. After a year, having generated less than 10 percent of the revenues generated by Kristen, we had no choice but to say goodbye. These decisions are always hard for me. Kristen's replacement was a kind, caring person who found herself in a position where she struggled to succeed. The decision was painful for all concerned.

We then hired a second replacement for Kristen. I continued to focus on creating and launching new initiatives with some of our past and current medical society partners. I also took on the added role of personally generating grant requests to increase revenues. It was a role with which I was quite familiar from my early days with the company. For the past fifteen years, however, it was one that was typically reserved for members of the grant team.

The second replacement, we soon learned, was also struggling. I continued to stress. Peace seemed so very far away. There were more prayers. I kept asking myself, "Why is this situation so different?

Why hasn't God answered my prayer?" I spent a great deal of time pondering this question.

My loving wife, Chris, saw the toll it was taking on me. One day she commented, "I miss the old Mikey."

In time, I came to recognize the problem, and the problem was me. I asked God to take control and give me peace while never loosening my grip on the wheel. Don't misunderstand me. I knew that God expected me to do my part and do it to the best of my ability. There was a great deal of work to be done. The important question was: am I willing to relinquish the control and ultimate outcome to our faithful and loving Lord? Was I willing to accept God's will in this, even if it was not the answer I wanted? To be honest, I must confess that the answer was no.

As I looked back to my cancer experience, I realized that after being told initially that my chances of survival might be fifty-fifty, I had to accept that there was little I could do to change the outcome. It was to some degree in the hands of the doctors caring for me, but ultimately, it was in the hands of God. Consequently, I turned it completely over to the Lord. In letting go and having faith in God, regardless of the outcome, I had total peace. I placed my trust in his plan, even if it meant he was going to bring me home.

That was certainly not the case with the situation with the company. It took time for me to come to terms with the truth.

Looking back, I realized that it was rooted, in part, to my childhood. As mentioned earlier, I struggled in school as a young child. Our constant moves made our family's life a bit like a roller coaster. Having switched schools seven times during my elementary school years, I was in a constant state of adjustment, struggling to catch up. I became more determined than ever to emerge from these challenges. I think this drive began to really take hold as I entered high school. I made the honor roll during the first semester of my freshman year. With this accomplishment, I became determined to remain on the honor roll for the balance of my high school education. Goal accomplished! I finished in the top 10 percent of my class and made the National Honor Society. Upon graduation, I was awarded a state scholarship, which entitled me to free tuition at any state-sponsored university in the state of New Jersey.

In my sophomore year of high school, I decided to try out for the wrestling team. After several weeks of practice, the decision was made. We all rushed to catch a glimpse of the bulletin board just outside the gym. Today they were announcing the final cuts for the wrestling team. I quickly looked down the list. Searching a second time, I realized that my name was missing. I was deeply disappointed yet still determined. I approached Coach Weir and asked if he would allow me to practice with the team. I wanted to be ready for the following season. To my surprise, he agreed.

After a month, he stopped the practice, stood before the team, and said, "I don't know if Mike Fullmer will ever be a great wrestler, but he has more heart than anyone in this room. For this reason, I'm adding Mike to our roster."

By my senior year, I was captain of that team and had the team's best record. At the conclusion of that year, the school awarded me with a trophy, recognizing me as the "most valuable player" in that sport.

My point is that I had become deeply driven by goals and determination. I would set my goals, map out my path, and drive myself toward achievement. This deeply seated internal drive helped lead me to the completion of my MBA while working in a full-time job. It helped take me down a successful forty-year career path in healthcare. This included launching my own business in continuing medical education some twenty-five years earlier. Chris and I took that step knowing that if it had failed, as many start-ups do in the first two years, we would have needed to sell the house and start all over again.

The drive and goal orientation had served me well, but was this truly the key reason for my successes? How much of it was the result of God's plan for me and his gifts to me? How many people had blessed and impacted my life, helping me along that path? Had I fully grasped the role of God and his plan for my life in each success? So often now, I thank God for his blessings in the various areas of my life. I have also come to realize that I can easily lose sight of his plan and will if my ultimate focus is on the achievement of my goals. It is critical to be seeking, trusting in, and submitting to his. It was a hard lesson I needed to learn and remember.

The bottom line is: are we willing to do our absolute best while fully submitting to and trusting in his will? As children of a faithful and loving God, love and trust become our calling in life. The closer we grow to him, the more we grow through him, and the clearer his will becomes. Sometimes it is not clear right away. It may require patience. He may take us in directions we never expected or perhaps never wanted. It is then and only then, as we fully embrace him, that we have true peace.

As a side note, I recently sold the business. The employees are all now gainfully employed, and I am once again fully retired. More importantly, I have been able to learn important lessons about submission and trust. I find my life to be an ongoing learning experience. At times I am sure God is looking down on me smiling and shaking his head. With this thought, I remind myself that we are all works in progress. As I seek him with all my heart, I grow. As I learn to trust in his will and his plan for my life, even in the most difficult circumstances, my heart more closely aligns with his. Only then will I find the peace, joy, and hope that God intended. In the end, I so look forward to one day being in his presence, a gift that will last forever.

> And I am sure of this, that he who began a good work in you will bring it to completion at the day of Jesus Christ. (Philippians 1:6 ESV)

May the Lord guide me and use me, despite my weaknesses and the things I have yet to learn. May I love you, Lord, with all my heart, trusting and submitting to your will for my life. Lord, help me to learn how to love as you love, loving you and others with all my heart. This is my prayer.

> I have fought the good fight, I have finished the race, I have kept the faith. (2 Timothy 4:7 ESV)

Acknowledgments

I wish to thank my wife, Chris, as she patiently allowed me to disappear into my office for countless hours while I poured myself into this book of reflection. I am also very thankful that I had her by my side as we jointly traveled this journey. I am particularly grateful for God's countless blessings along the way, which included the presence of my love and life partner. I came so close to losing her.

We are both incredibly grateful for the countless friends and family members who supported us with love, phone calls, emails, visits, and prayers throughout these many trials.

I also wish to thank Rev. Dr. Jerry Schmoyer, Rev. David Gilbert, and Kathy Cooper for their insights and input as I took the draft manuscript through its late-stage review process.

Above all, I want to thank our Lord, Father, our loving Savior, Jesus, and the Holy Spirit. Our Lord patiently led us, taught us, refined us, strengthened us, and deeply loved us through it all. Your promises never fail. You are the source of our hope and joy. I am an imperfect work in progress, but I have been blessed beyond measure.